Social Media in Healthcare Information

Social Media in Healthcare Information

Paula Younger

facet publishing

Published by Facet Publishing
c/o British Library, 96 Euston Road, London NW1 2DB
www.facetpublishing.co.uk

Facet Publishing is wholly owned by CILIP: the Library and Information Association.

British Library Cataloguing in Publication Data
A catalogue record for this book is available from the British Library.

ISBN 978-1-78330-678-7 (paperback)
ISBN 978-1-78330-679-4 (hardback)
ISBN 978-1-78330-680-0 (PDF)
ISBN 978-1-78330-681-7 (EPUB)

First published 2025

MIX
Paper | Supporting responsible forestry
FSC® C013604
www.fsc.org

The manufacturer's authorised representative in the EU for product safety is Logos Europe, 9 rue Nicolas Poussin, 17000 La Rochelle, France (contact@logoseurope.eu, www.logoseurope.eu).

Typeset from author's files in 10/13pt Palatino and OpenSans by Flagholme Publishing Services.
Printed and made in Great Britain by CPI Group (UK) Ltd, Croydon, CR0 4YY..

Contents

About the Author

Paula Younger has spent most of her library career in healthcare libraries in the UK, with experience of the NHS, higher education and the Ministry of Defence. Roles have included Electronic Resources Librarian, Clinical Librarian and Library Manager. She has a long-standing interest in how technology is being used and how it can be used to enhance healthcare information. She is currently Library Manager at Wrightington, Wigan and Leigh NHS Teaching Hospitals in Greater Manchester.

Introduction

In a world where so many of our daily transactions and tasks depend on it, it can be difficult to remember what life was like before the arrival of the internet. It's not surprising that it can sometimes feel as if the internet has always been with us. That perception is, however, misleading.

Social media is a relatively recent internet development, although the principles of the network as a platform for social interactivity can be seen right from the start. While there were huge steps forward in the 1960s that set the scene for our modern internet, it wasn't until around the mid-to-late 1990s that this 'network of computer networks' showed signs of becoming the powerhouse and essential life tool it is today. It's generally agreed that the World Wide Web was created by Tim Berners-Lee in 1989 during his time at the Conseil Européen pour la Recherche Nucléaire (better known as CERN).

The internet as we know it is, therefore, about as old as one human generation. From its origins, when it was mostly the preserve of defence and research, the 'information superhighway' or simply the internet has become an essential and almost unavoidable feature of our everyday lives. At the time of writing, in the mid-2020s, it has become an integral part of banking, education, travel, our working lives and almost every aspect of daily life.

In the early days of the internet's development, users were often happy to share content, frequently for little or no financial reward. As internet usage figures grew to millions of users from the mid-1990s onwards, however, content providers soon began trying to establish how this potential goldmine could be monetised.

Blogs, podcasts, RSS feeds, wikis and above all social networking platforms are examples of the underlying software that has made these new levels of collaboration and socialisation possible – all Web 2.0 technologies. In a move that echoed the origins of the internet itself, where no one organisation or person had overall control, the thinking behind many Web 2.0 software developments in their early stages was that anyone would be able to add, edit and share or reuse content. Although this is still the case, much of that content has now been monetised. While free versions of many of the platforms remain available, this often comes at a non-financial cost. Many companies will pay a premium to advertise their products and services to a target audience they think is likely to use those products or services.

Social networking and social media, alongside ever more powerful mobile technology, have played a huge part in the spread and utilisation of the internet. Where mobile communication technology is widely used, it has been found to influence the quality of face-to-face conversations, resulting in altered traditional communication patterns (Przybylski and Weinstein, 2017). Anyone who has ever had to attempt to decipher text messages concocted by younger generations will attest to the effect text speak (or txtspk if you prefer) has had on the English language and others.

Definitions of social media: the role of Web 2.0

The way in which we use what is currently called social media is a world away from the origins of the internet, if not in intention, then certainly in application. Any discussion of social media use requires a tacit – or clearly stated – understanding of the Web 2.0 technologies that make social media possible.

Despite the fact that Web 2.0 technologies have been with us for well over a decade at the time of writing, Gross (2012) is one of many authors who point out that the definition remains somewhat nebulous. Although the first use of the term is often attributed to Tim O'Reilly of O'Reilly Media at a conference in 2004, some sources believe that the term was coined far earlier, in 1999 by Darcy DiNucci (Aced, 2013).

The potential use of Web 2.0 for communication took a huge step forward when mobile phones with internet capability became affordable and widespread. There was another 'quantum leap' when what we currently call smartphones hit the market and gradually became both more powerful and more affordable.

The point at which 'social media' became part of the English language and the definition of the term are also slightly nebulous. In their systematic review Aichner et al. (2021) outline how the definition of social media changed between 1994 and 2019. In 88 potential papers, the terms 'social network' or 'social networks' occurred more commonly in the literature they studied than 'social media' or 'social networking'. The first formal definition in the review dates to Wellman in 1996, who used the term 'computer-supported social networks'. For Garton, Haythornthwaite and Wellman in 1997, a computer network that connected either people or organisations was a 'social network' and by 2006, Acquisti and Gross described online social networks as 'an internet community where individuals interact'. Aichner et al. (2021) discovered that 'virtual community' was the term used most often between 1997 and 2002, while 'social network' was found most frequently in research from 2005 to 2009. It wasn't until around 2010 that 'social media' became the most frequently used term: a useful fact when tracking down research in the area (Aichner et al., 2021).

Specific social media platforms and methods of communication underpinned by Web 2.0 technologies include, but are not limited to: Facebook; X (formerly known as Twitter); YouTube; TikTok; Snapchat; Reddit; Instagram; Vimeo; WhatsApp; podcasts; vodcasts; wikis; and blogs (Kanchan and Gaidhane, 2023). All of these encourage communication between those who make use of them, offering the opportunity for interactions around the world.

Figures for 2023 reveal that, on average, we spend almost three and a half hours a day on our phones in the UK, while in the USA it was more than four and a half hours. In almost every walk of life, during any five-minute period, at least a third of those around you will be intent on the content on their phones at some point. While it can sometimes feel as if we now live our entire lives through the prism of social media and are permanently glued to our smartphones, it's only a few years since either made an appearance.

With the arrival of affordable smartphones with huge amounts of processing power and, crucially, integrated cameras, microphones and multimedia capability, the world as we knew it changed dramatically. Once the wireless connection standard we commonly refer to as Wi-Fi became both affordable and widespread, the scene was set for 'internet anywhere'. Social networking became a major method of communicating and interacting, although at the time of writing one of the most commonly used terms is social media (Aichner et al., 2021).

The development of social media

Although some authors put the arrival of what is now often termed 'social media' rather earlier (McIntyre, 2014; Dhingra and Mudgal, 2019), one view is that the phenomenon began in around 1997, with the advent of the social networking site 'SixDegrees' (Winder, 2007). The company was named after the 'six degrees of separation' theory, generally believed to have originated with Stanley Milgram in the 1960s, which posits that between any two people, links will be found within 'six degrees' of people they are somehow connected to as individuals. SixDegrees.com is usually regarded as the first true social media platform. Users were allowed to create profiles, maintain friends lists and make contact through the private messaging system on the site – features which we now take for granted in most modern social media apps.

Given that the original purposes of social media platforms and technology developments were for communities to share information, it is not surprising that Baym (2015) is one of those who concludes that all communication media are, at base, intrinsically social. Research over many years has repeatedly shown that humans are, often, 'inherently' social (Young, 2008). Social media can be regarded as a modern iteration of this need.

Whether social media influences us or we influence social media is a moot point. Some commentators, such as Miller et al. (2016) would argue that the world has also changed social media. We have certainly come a long way since the early days of social networks like SixDegrees, Friends Reunited and MySpace.

Despite the fact that there are now at least two generations who have never known a world without the internet, the internet is still evolving. From its research and defence system beginnings, this network of computer networks has become a global platform for communication; sharing ideas; education; and finding like-minded groups of people.

Social media in healthcare information: why now?

After just over a decade of development and evolution, this is a particularly apposite time to look at how social media is currently used in healthcare information provision. Healthcare is one of the areas where social media has had – and still has – a measurable effect in both positive and negative ways. Although the majority of the examples in the book are UK-based, in our globalised world many of the information concerns are equally applicable to other geographics and settings.

This includes a consideration of how it is used in research, education, health promotion and the dissemination of public health messages. When it comes to public health messages, consideration of misinformation in social media is a major issue, coming to a peak during the COVID-19 pandemic that began in 2019–20 and in the aftermath.

Along with misinformation, there are other ethical aspects to the use of social media that need to be managed. User educators and healthcare researchers are two groups that are particularly affected by ethical considerations. This is one of many areas where healthcare information professionals can utilise their skills to help guide healthcare professionals through the information ethical maze. There are also particular considerations explored in Chapter 8 around security of information, an evergreen topic.

The use of social media by information professionals

Information professionals may also find social media of immense use for continuing professional development, networking and as an option to help translate 'traditional' library skills into a more modern form. Skills of information curation, metadata, marketing and critical appraisal all offer ways for information professionals to connect with and educate users. Social media also offers a way for healthcare information professionals to remotely participate in continuing professional development (CPD) opportunities such as conferences and webinars.

Social media during the COVID-19 pandemic

There are times when technology and society take huge leaps forward and social media is no exception. There were what could be termed quantum leaps forward in the way social media was used in healthcare information during the COVID-19 pandemic of 2020 to 2022. While misinformation is one serious aspect of the use of social media at this time, social media also offered public health organisations a rapid and cost-effective way of trying to ensure that their own evidence-based messages, calls to vaccination and information about preventative measures were distributed.

Social media: underlying core principles for librarians

In his *The Five Laws of Library Science* (1931), S. R. Ranganathan, regarded as the 'father' of library science, came up with five laws that can easily be adapted to the online healthcare world, including the way we use social media.

The first law, 'Books are for use', can become 'Social media [is] for use', while 'Every person his or her book' becomes 'Every person his or her [social media platform]' and 'Every book its reader' turns into 'Every [social media post/platform] its reader'.

When it comes to the next two laws, particularly saving the reader's time and accepting that a library is a 'growing organism', the application to social media is extremely clear. At its best, social media can offer us extraordinarily time-efficient ways of finding out what is happening in a particular field, or a very efficacious way of communicating with users, peers and potential users. In addition, social media behaves somewhat like an organism. It grows; it dies back; it evolves; it may even regenerate and bloom again, if that term can be applied to an online system or communications channel.

How this book is structured

This book offers a snapshot of the state of social media in healthcare information at the time of writing. Chapters 1 and 2 provide the basics of the development of the internet and Web 2.0, the technologies that underlie social media. Chapters 3, 4 and 5 take more in-depth looks at social media in healthcare settings, including healthcare research and medical education, while Chapter 6 explores the role of social media in the misinformation so prevalent around COVID-19. Chapter 7 looks at some of the barriers to the use of social media in healthcare information. In Chapter 8, some of the main ethical, moral and legal considerations of using social media in healthcare information come under scrutiny. Some potential future developments in social media are theorised in Chapter 9, with the Conclusion drawing the themes of the book together.

In the chapters that follow, the focus is on those social media platforms which are used most often in healthcare settings. The overall aim is to offer a snapshot of a time when social media has become so embedded in our lives that it is almost impossible to avoid, for good or bad, unless we make a conscious effort to do so.

At this point, we also stand on the brink of a new technological revolution: artificial intelligence (AI). In practice, this is currently often used to refer mostly to Large Language Models (LLMs) such as ChatGPT and Google's Gemini (a successor to Bard). There are, however, other burgeoning AI technologies which may or may not have a direct impact on the work of healthcare information professionals and the healthcare professional community that we support. The impacts of AI on patients and service users are also currently in their infancy, although there is already an awareness that critical thinking skills in the general population need to be improved when using this new technology (Carucci, 2024).

As well as outlining some of the main ways in which social media underpins, facilitates and sometimes hinders the effective provision of healthcare information, there will be consideration of the roles of information professionals in that context.

The book is not a practical instruction manual on how to set up social media accounts and use them; support of that kind is probably best found on the internet itself, given the rapid and frequent changes to social media. Suggestions are, however, woven through each chapter to include methods for the incorporation of the platforms and apps into the everyday work of healthcare professionals and healthcare information professionals. There are also examples of how social media platforms and approaches have been used throughout the chapters.

Although the majority of the examples in the book are UK-based, the issues around social media in healthcare apply to many other geographies and settings. This will be particularly clear in the chapter on misinformation during COVID-19. Many of the approaches, concerns and situations outlined are global. They have come into existence almost as a side effect of social media and how it has changed the way in which we interact with one another and the internet.

This book is not a history of social media in healthcare either, although several of the chapters inevitably incorporate a brief historical overview, including the development of the internet in general. Throughout it will be apparent that it is the underlying Web 2.0 technology that has allowed social media to evolve to its current point. Consequently, an understanding of some of those principles, and how Web 2.0 has been used in healthcare settings, will benefit healthcare information professionals immensely.

Finally, this book is not a second edition of *Using Web 2.0 for Health Information* (Younger and Morgan, 2011), although there is some thematic crossover and some of the topics from that publication are updated in this text. In those cases, what will be apparent is how far the past 14–15 years have taken us.

The future of social media in healthcare

The book concludes (Chapter 9) with an attempt to look into the future, although this is always fraught with uncertainty and it is, of course, always extremely easy to show wisdom with the benefit of hindsight. While the past is not always as clear a guide to the future as some historians would like us to believe, the skills and knowledge that we have acquired while grappling with Web 2.0 will be equally useful in social media and beyond.

We may, however, find ourselves able to discern some trends on social media and the accompanying AI and Internet of Things which are likely to continue and expand, if we maintain our current trajectory. These developments are likely to include virtual reality and augmented reality, as well as the possible development of the Semantic Web and/or the Internet of Things.

A small number of titles are available that explore the use of social media from a purely healthcare or purely patient perspective. There are none, however, at the time of writing, that explore how social media has an impact on the work of healthcare librarians or how healthcare information professionals have incorporated it into their practice.

CHAPTER 1

The Internet: The Story So Far

The evolution of the internet

Whenever we want to understand where we are and how we got here, taking a brief look at history can be invaluable, especially in a world where the internet is now so ubiquitous that its origins have almost faded into myth. There are now generations of individuals who have never known a world without the internet. Effectively, that means the majority of those born post-1994.

As with all life-changing inventions, the internet as we know it at present owes a great deal of its development to previous inventions and discoveries. These include the telephone, radio and television.

Developments in the progress of the internet can often be 'grouped' by years or decades. Long before the internet was even a twinkle of an idea, there were many real-world analogue proposals to create a physical representation of all the knowledge in the world. The concept of the internet, or at least of an immense repository of human knowledge, has been predicted in literature and the arts for centuries.

Imagining the internet

In 1728, when Ephraim Chambers published his *Cyclopaedia,* articles were linked through cross-references, an early real-world forerunner of the hyperlink. For Paul Otlet and Henri La Fontaine, the Universal Decimal Classification was central to their *Mundaneum* proposal (Hanlon, 2008). This central repository of global knowledge was followed, in 1934, by Otlet's vision for the 'Radiated Library', where phones retrieved information before transmitting it as television signals.

Science fiction has often predicted future developments in technology, with H. G. Wells one of those who often led the field. His 'World Brain' was conceptualised as a central knowledge repository that anyone could access. The Memex in 'As We May Think' by Vannevar Bush, published in 1945, again made use of links in a personal information repository. Other works of fiction that foresaw the internet, or something very close to it, include *Neuromancer*, a 1984 novel by William Gibson and, many decades earlier, an 1898 short story by Mark Twain called *From the 'London Times' of 1904*.

The 1950s to the mid-1980s

In popular culture today the 1950s are often presented to us as a contrast to our own technology-heavy times, and as a bastion of traditional values with a slower pace of life than our modern age, while in fact the years that followed the end of World War 2 saw many advances in science. This included great leaps forward in computing science. While many of us know the name Tim Berners-Lee in connection with the internet milestone of creating the World Wide Web, his mother, Mary Lee Berners-Lee (née Woods) was also a pioneer of computing. She was responsible for setting up the first general-purpose computer that became commercially available, the Ferranti Mark 1 in 1951.

Nine years later, in 1960, a network of computers providing library functions along with advanced methods of retrieving information was envisioned by J. C. R. Licklider. Licklider was both a psychologist and a computer scientist and is generally considered to be one of the most important figures in the history of computer science. His input enabled the ARPANET, the direct ancestor of the internet: he was amongst the first to envisage an interconnected network of machines.

From 1960 to 1969, networking continued to be a major focus, from the papers on packet switching of data published by Paul Baran to the work of Leonard Kleinrock that led to the foundation of the ARPANET. When Licklider became the director of the Information Processing Techniques Office at the Advanced Research Projects Agency (ARPA), his aim was to create a computer network that was 'intergalactic' in scope, although the ARPANET as such was not proposed until 1966 by Robert Taylor. The previous year, computer scientist Lawrence (or Larry) Roberts and his fellow MIT scientist Thomas Merrill had connected computers over a wide-area network, or WAN.

Another major milestone came in 1968. Bolt, Beranek and Newman, Inc. (now known as the research and development company Raytheon BBN) was contracted to ARPA to develop what was known as the Interface Message Processor (IMP) – an ancestor of our modern routers. The mid-1960s to the early 1990s were a time for further developments in e-mail and hypertext, with inventor Douglas Engelbart demonstrating the first hypertext system in 1968. He also patented the computer mouse. We have a lot to thank him for –

without his work on input devices we'd still be limited to trying to control computers via electric switches or punched cards.

At the time of its inception in the 1960s, the internet was relatively one-dimensional. By modern standards, there was little opportunity for interaction beyond text-based bulletin boards. When e-mail was invented in 1971 by Ray Tomlinson, the communication enabled by the internet became far more interactive. Tomlinson worked as a computer engineer at Bolt, Beranek and Newman in the USA. Various protocols that we would still recognise today followed, many of which facilitated the capacity of computers and networks to 'talk' to each other. TCP/IP, the brainchild of Bob Kahn and Vint Cerf in 1973, offered a chance to standardise communication protocols on the internet. If you've ever had cause to delve into the router settings on your device, you'll know this protocol is still in use today.

Following the invention of e-mail, the internet began to take a shape that we would recognise today. When Michael Hart launched Project Gutenberg in 1971, he effectively invented the e-book. Even today, this collection of online public domain texts and other literature makes extensive use of text and hyperlinks and is supported by a vast network of volunteers.

Computing continued to develop during the 1970s and 1980s, with personal computers in particular effectively 'changing the game'. This is despite IBM Chairman Thomas Watson famously declaring in 1943 that the world market could bear maybe 'five computers'.

It was with the unstoppable rise of the World Wide Web that the internet began to take shape as a modern, interactive, multimedia environment, albeit one that was still tethered to desktop computers. Rather than attempt to retrieve lists and information about content on the internet via directories, users were suddenly able to use a 'graphical user interface' (GUI) incorporating images and easy-to-read text. The American businessman and former software engineer Marc Andreessen had released the first popular GUI web browser, Mosaic, in 1993. Ordinary users were able to interact with information on the internet with relative ease.

The 1990s: the coming of the search engine

The first search engine was Archie in 1990, although due to the limited amount of content on the internet, at that point Archie only retrieved listings of files available rather than actual content. Tim Berners-Lee followed this up in 1991 with his Virtual Library, allowing users to find URLs for different websites. The library was hosted by the web servers at Conseil Européen pour la Recherche Nucléaire (CERN) in Geneva.

Originally hosted by the University of Stirling, JumpStation then created a linear search which showed both title and header of a page in the same results. Results were ranked in the order they were found. Writer Jonathon Fletcher graduated from the University in 1992 and has subsequently often been described as the 'father of the search engine'. Unfortunately at the time he was unable to attract further investment or backing to develop the concept.

Between 1994 to 1998, the internet saw the appearance of several search engines, some of which are still with us, although their appearance may have changed. Yahoo! Search, created by David Filo and Jerry Yang, and WebCrawler appeared in 1994, along with Lycos. Other search engines included AskJeeves, Inktomi and Excite.

Then, in 1996, Larry Page and Sergey Brin set the scene for internet search as we currently know it. Page and Brin created what became the predecessor to Google, BackRub. Websites began taking backlinks to a site from other websites and introduced the concept of ranking the original website in a method that improved the search. When one website links to another website, this is regarded as a vote. This helps to provide the basis for the 'authority' of a website – a concept that still underpins the search algorithms we use today.

Once Google itself arrived on the scene in 1998 and rapidly became the search engine of choice, the fate of civilisation was set. It had reached one billion pages just two years later. Wikipedia, the crowdsourced online encyclopaedia that anyone can edit or correct, was also widely used by around 2007. While Google is primarily a search engine, Wikipedia is usually regarded as the world's largest and most well-known wiki.

By the mid-2010s, there were over 3 billion people using the internet – just under half the world's population at the time of 6.725 billion (Worldometer, 2025).

Personal computers and the dot.com bubble

In the mid to late 1990s new technologies became especially widespread.

Towards the end of the decade, stock market valuations of many technology-focused companies reached unprecedented levels. What became known as dot.com start-ups were hailed as one of the major success stories of our age. One starting point for the dot.com movement was arguably the Initial Public Offering (IPO) of the Netscape browser in 1995.

Although transitions are rarely as exact or short as some history books would like us to believe, in retrospect the dot.com bubble represents a marker from one version of the web to the next. In around the mid-1990s, banner advertisements and other commercial web activities also became widespread. This is a feature many of us would recognise from social media today, particularly the free or basic versions, which often track personal data usually for the sake of marketing. After all, if you're not sure what the product is, it's probably you (Goodson, 2012).

The dot.com bubble burst, however, as stock market bubbles generally do at some point, in 2001. The fallout was dramatic. The event encompassed losses of billions of dollars and thousands of failed companies and lost livelihoods.

The mid-1990s to the mid-2010s

Both the mid-1990s and the mid-2010s were particularly significant periods in terms of how the internet developed.

The year 2014 saw the 45th anniversary of the first ARPANET link that was, effectively, the birth of the internet. This link had been established on 29 October 1969 and linked computers at the University of California Los Angeles (UCLA) and Stanford Research Institute (SRI), now known as SRI International. (Anyone who has struggled with connectivity in a healthcare institution might like to know that the first message attempt crashed.)

The same year, 2014, included another significant anniversary. While healthcare information professionals may know MeSH as the term for the medical taxonomy that helps us search the literature effectively and efficiently, fewer people know (or remember) that it was the original name Tim Berners-Lee came up with in March 1989 for what we now know as the World Wide Web (Miller, 2014).

While the internet can be regarded as a network infrastructure, the World Wide Web can be thought of as a software infrastructure – the next layer of the internet cake, if you like.

The arrival of Web 2.0

In the wake of the 'dot.com crash', as it came to be known, Web 2.0 was a term often used to group together the emerging new technologies. If Web 1.0 belonged, largely, to corporate organisations, Web 2.0 was squarely in the hands of the individual and communities, at least in the early days of its development. Technologies still in use today that we would recognise as coming under the Web 2.0 heading emphasise online collaboration, the building of communities and social networking.

The coming of the smartphone

While social media was popular even when the most common ways of accessing it were via desktops and laptops, it became a global phenomenon following the arrival of the smartphone in the mid-1990s.

On 16 August 1994, IBM Simon was released, often regarded as the first smartphone. It featured a combined phone, address book, calculator, calendar and notepad and, crucially, a touchscreen. Suddenly, it was no longer necessary to have a keyboard attached to be able to access the internet. Ericsson's R380 release on 19 June 2000 was, however, the first device that was explicitly labelled as a 'smartphone'.

Then came the mighty Nokia 7650 in October 2001. For many years, the Nokia name was synonymous with mobile phones and smartphones, although the BlackBerry smartphone gave them a run for their money with the 5810.

Palm and Motorola followed with their devices, before, in 2007, Steve Jobs released the first iPhone on an unsuspecting world. Not only did the device have a touchscreen, the interface was actually touchscreen-centric. A year later, the first Android Smartphone was released, the HTC Dream (T-Mobile G1), signifying the entry of Google onto the market.

Later releases of the iPhone followed, with new Android phones hot on their heels, including the Samsung Galaxy S in 2010. In 2011, Nokia and Microsoft announced their major partnership, with yet another operating system, Windows Phone. One issue with many of the earlier mobile phones, however, was the speed of the processor. When the HTC One X was launched in 2012, its far faster quad-core heralded a major advance in mobile computing power.

A forerunner of the smartphone was the Personal Digital Assistant, or PDA, which also showed great promise initially but has subsequently been mostly overtaken by smartphone developments. In the early years of Web 2.0, ownership of personal PDAs amongst clinicians was relatively high (Divall, Camosso-Stefinovic and Baker, 2013), with Baumgart (2005) outlining the possibilities for clinicians to make use of the new technology to work with their patients and service users. By 2015, almost 99% of doctors and just over 95% of nurses owned a smartphone, with over 92% of doctors and over 53% of nurses describing them as either 'very useful' or 'useful' as an assisting tool to help with their clinical duties (Mobasheri et al., 2015).

The smartphone: further developments

Further smartphone developments have followed that have set the scene for the technology we know – and sometimes love – today. In 2024, we take Alexa (or Echo, Amazon, Computer, or Ziggy if you prefer) and other digital voice activated systems (or assistants) for granted, but it wasn't until 2011 that Apple announced Siri. The age of AI in smartphones had begun.

Google's own Pixel arrived on 29 September 2015 and when Samsung released their Galaxy S7 Edge in March 2016, the built-in capability for photography in lower levels of light made it an attractive proposition for those who loved to take an impromptu snap or two.

With the arrival of the first foldable phone, the Samsung Galaxy Fold, in 2019, phones became smaller and, often, thinner and lighter. And in autumn 2020, Apple's iPhone 12 took a leap forward to incorporate 5G mobile technology.

Smartphones, social media and health

Smartphones are tailor-made for social media; or, in an alternative reading, many forms of modern social media are designed around the smartphone. This combination of portability and versatility can be a heady mix.

As 5G mobile communication networks become more widespread in many – but not all – parts of the world, phones continue to become thinner and lighter and, crucially, battery life improves; these tiny devices allow us to carry more computing power in our bag or pocket than our 1960s predecessors would have believed.

Smartphones have not, however, been without their controversy. This is not just due to the limits on battery life or the ease with which we can now be tracked. There were known issues around the explosion of the Galaxy Note 7, for example, highlighted in autumn 2016, which resulted in a global recall of the device.

The impact of smartphones on individual health, however, particularly mental health, is another area of emerging research. Smartphone addiction is a recognised phenomenon and has been since at least the early 2010s (Salehan and Negahban, 2013). When designing or participating in social media interactions, healthcare information professionals need to be aware that 'likes' and other measures of engagement on the platforms can result in a dopamine hit, like any other addiction. Several subsequent commentators around the world have explored the issue (Carter et al., 2024; Subramaniam et al., 2024; Jahagirdar et al., 2021).

Smartphones can nevertheless offer potential as a force for good in healthcare information. They have, for example, been used to report adverse drug events in low-resource settings (Dubale et al., 2024); track disease-specific health literacy in China (Chen et al., 2024); and assess the usefulness of breathing exercises incorporated into health apps to help with symptoms of stress (Schleicher et al., 2024).

The next chapter looks at defining the context of social media in general, with an overview of some of the most commonly used platforms and apps.

CHAPTER 2

What is Social Media?

Introduction

In 1994, there were an estimated 20 million internet users around the world. By 2008, this number was more than 1.5 billion (World Bank, 2011) and at the time of writing, there are an estimated 5.35 billion people online (around 66.2% of the global population (Liu, Amin and Stemmler, 2024).) In 2023 alone there were approximately 97 million new users. Alongside the UK and the USA, the countries which dominate this picture of internet usage include European countries Norway, Denmark, Sweden and Finland, and Middle East locations Bahrain, Kuwait, Qatar, Saudi Arabia and the United Arab Emirates. Despite their large populations, India and China still have a high proportion of citizens who are not connected. At the bottom of the table is North Korea, where access to the internet is estimated to be below 10% of the country's population (Kemp, 2024).

The internet rapidly became an information tool of choice for many in its early days, before evolving into the interactive virtual social environment that we know today.

The mid-1990s were a pivotal time for internet development, when the mainly text-based information environment transformed and new interactive sites appeared at a rapid pace. In 1994, the first sale on Echo Bay's Auction Bay took place. This online marketplace was a forerunner of eBay (eBay, 2023). Not only could users trade items, it was also possible to exchange e-mails and an important feature was the ability to rate transactions, thereby enabling buyers and sellers to achieve approval scores.

The increasing interactive functionality of the internet over the last 30 years has changed much of society, particularly the ways in which we communicate with each other, almost beyond recognition (Naughton, 2016). This has been apparent from at least the mid-1990s, when free e-mail services became a feature of the internet landscape, with Hotmail changing the way we communicate in 1996 and setting the stage for our e-mail-dependent world (Gibbs, 2016). Two years earlier, in 1994, graphical web browsers had opened up the internet to make it accessible and interactive, although the general release to the unsuspecting public of the current search engine behemoth, Google, was still four years in the future (Ray, 2024).

Web 1.0 to Web 3.0

Web 1.0 was occasionally used as the internet emerged, although it has been adopted as more of a retrospective term now. O'Reilly (2005) found Web 1.0 to be didactic in nature, offering less of an interactive user experience than the subsequent Web 2.0 environment. O'Reilly and Battelle (2009) came up with an elegant description of Web 2.0 as 'harnessing collective intelligence'.

Some associated terms, such as Health 2.0 and Library 2.0, have now been incorporated into the English language, at least in some specialised areas (Boxen, 2008). For Hinchcliffe (2006), however, the term Web 2.0 was just jargon. Not long after this judgement, the term 'Web 2.0' became the one-millionth official term in the English language in 2009 (Topping, 2009).

O'Reilly and Battelle (2009) referred to their vision as 'Web as platform'. They correctly forecast a more collaborative approach to content, with software applications that took advantage of the burgeoning increased connectivity of the internet. Users were moving away from data and applications that sat on the desktop to those that were either in 'the cloud' (shared online spaces), accessible via mobile technology, or both.

Crucially, the new applications that began to appear at this time were extremely easy to use. This made them accessible to users with very basic levels of ICT literacy. Creating blog posts, entries in wikis, social bookmarks, or mashups (where content is incorporated from different sources) were now within reach of those without specialised programming skills or knowledge.

Web 2.0 and social media

Although Google Search is generally not regarded as a Web 2.0 development, many other Google products have Web 2.0 features, for example Google Docs, Google Slides and Google Sheets, all of which lend themselves well to collaborative document creation. When new computer software is released, version numbering is usually used, starting with 1.0, progressing to 2.0, 2.1, 2.2 and so on. The phrases Web 1.0 and Web 2.0 reference this, with Web 3.0 used occasionally as a way of describing the probable next stage of the internet.

Web 2.0 and social media are often used interchangeably, although social media is, technically, underpinned by Web 2.0 technologies. Social media has uses beyond simple exchanges of messages or even multimedia clips. It also allows users to effectively construct their own learning environment, connected in a way that allows them to interact socially and collaborate with others over long distances, even globally. Social media allows users to gain access whenever they require it to resources and knowledge on a collective level.

This can be particularly valuable for the otherwise potentially isolated solo librarian seeking to pursue CPD opportunities and peer support. For many solo librarians, or those in very small services, time and funding are both of the essence. It may not be easy for them to carve out opportunities to attend conferences or even short courses (Kendrick, Leaver and Tritt, 2013). Social media offers a practical solution (Luo and Hostetler, 2020; Broady-Preston, 2009).

Another aspect of Web 2.0 applications and solutions which remains very evident in our cloud-based environment is the ease of access from any internet-enabled device. That may mean a desktop, laptop, smartphone or other mobile device. Regalado (2011) is one of many authors who date the coining of the term 'cloud computing' to 1996, although it came into more widespread use in around 2006.

The move towards cloud computing also foreshadowed the move from powerful desktop-based machines to a world where the capacity at which a network is able to transmit data became one of the most important factors in the development of the internet. Imbens and Kalyanaraman (2009) were amongst those who foresaw future iterations of the internet would require this increased bandwidth, compared to the localised investment in hardware associated with Web 1.0.

Defining social media

If Web 1.0 was the early, relatively one-dimensional internet, where content was produced and users typically consumed it and Web 2.0 was a second incarnation, where users began to use the internet as a communication channel, how can we define social media?

Although authors have different viewpoints and definitions, there is a consensus that it is difficult to define. According to Aichner et al. (2021), the term has been in use since 1994, when it was first used in an online environment called Matisse in Tokyo.

Over time, the term has come to describe a 'variety of online platforms, including blogs, business networks, collaborative projects, enterprise social networks (SN), forums, microblogs, photo sharing, products review, social bookmarking, social gaming, SN, video sharing and virtual worlds' (Aichner and Jacob, 2015). For Dol et al. (2019), social media encompasses 'interactive internet-based applications that enable users to share information, network and collaborate on the Web'.

Other terms that are sometimes used include 'virtual communities', 'social networks', 'social networking services', 'online social network', 'social networking sites' and 'social network sites' (Aichner and Jacob, 2015). Occasionally the abbreviations SM or SoMe are seen. For the purposes of this book, in most cases, the term 'social media' will be used.

In 2024, social media platforms are some of the most commonly used sources on the internet – or elsewhere – for both acquiring information and disseminating it. They offer one of the fastest methods for building awareness in the public health field amongst other related areas (Thelwall and Thelwall, 2020).

Although most platforms share several characteristics, it is possible to group them into categories. For Aichner and Jacob (2015), social media (or SM) describes a range of online platforms. These include but are not limited to blogs and microblogs, business networks and forums, photo and video sharing, product reviews and collaborative projects. The key is collaboration.

The rise of the social network

Friendster

In the early days of social media, social networking to link individuals, groups, companies, organisations and communities was a major objective. The now defunct Friendster was one of the earliest social networking sites to achieve generally widespread popularity. When Friendster was first released, the aim was that it would compete with Match.com, then one of the most popular dating sites in the world. Friendster evolved, however, to connect a wider community. It served as a way to connect friends who could exchange messages.

In a development similar to the fate of online community GeoCities, the focus of Friendster shifted towards Asia. It was particularly popular in Malaysia, the Philippines and Singapore, before rebranding itself as a social gaming site in 2011. Once it moved away from serving as a social networking platform, many user blogs, messages and photos were deleted. This is something of a hazard on social media, which by its nature has many platforms and posts that are very ephemeral. In some cases, this is deliberate. Instagram, the live photo messaging site, is one of those known for deleting stories and accounts unexpectedly, while Snapchat is deliberately designed for those wishing to send images and video clips with a short 'shelf life'.

Notwithstanding the fact that it was most popular with young adults, the overall user base for Friendster incorporated users from different backgrounds and age groups. Friendster users had walls where photos could be shared and friends discovered via connections, all features which are now typical of sites like Facebook, still the most widely used platform in the world. Friendster was especially popular in the USA, with high levels of popularity among young adults.

Even today, demographic analyses show that different age groups prefer different social media platforms – a key factor to remember when it comes to healthcare information and how we can help users access evidence-based, robust knowledge.

Despite its early success, Friendster gradually became slow and less responsive, resulting in high levels of frustration amongst users. After Friendster met its end in 2015, it had a significant influence on the social networking sites that came after it, including the mighty Facebook.

The Facebook

In its early days Facebook was more robust than Friendster, with better features and functionality. Originally called 'The Facebook' and started as a website for Harvard University students, Facebook is now a behemoth amongst social media sites and has managed to retain its pole position for decades. Most of its features, at least the basic aspects, remain free to use, with users creating their own pages. The main site of a user, whether an individual, company, business, or organisation is known as their profile. It remains one of the most popular sites for general social networking, with around 2.9 billion active users each month.

Common characteristics of social media platforms and sites

Most social media platforms share several common characteristics. These include allowing users to construct a profile of themselves that is public or at least partially public, with the option to restrict to other approved network users. Social media users are also able to curate or outline a list of other users to whom they are connected; upload and share content; and connect with other people via messaging systems.

Several sites incorporate another feature commonly found on social media platforms, namely that users or customers can give immediate feedback to content in the form of likes or comments. They can also pose questions, usually expecting quick and relatively personalised responses and share content, either their own 'user-generated content', or that of others.

Customers have also become, effectively, unpaid marketers and advocates for organisations, posting images, text and even videos to help build a corporate brand or organisational reputation – or to destroy it.

As well as an important tool allowing customers or service users to communicate with organisations, social media has also evolved into a communication modality commonly used for families, friends and co-workers or others as well as those with a common interest. One of the key features is that users can generate their own content – in fact, are expected to, even if this takes the form of merely sharing content.

While 'user-generated content' or UGC is a term commonly used in modern analyses of social media, this was not the case in earlier research. Until about 2009, the most important social media links were usually a by-product of common hobbies or interests. Even the terms used to describe how content found its way onto social media changed. Following 2010, the word used was most commonly 'share' rather than the 'upload' or 'exchange' which had appeared prior to that time. Whether the change or the language comes first is something of a moot point, although for those wishing to conduct further research into this area, Aichner et al. suggest that it may help to bear in mind that there is no single or even generally accepted definition.

Some types of social media platforms and approaches are, however, fairly well defined by now.

Blogs

Blogs are well known today as websites that are regularly updated with short, often topical, pieces, usually on a common theme, or for a particular audience. It was in 1997 that 'blog' entered the English language as a noun and the short form of 'weblog', coined by Peter Merholz and Jorn Barger respectively. It was Pyra Labs' Evan Williams who used the word 'blog' as both a noun and a verb, coming up with the word 'blogger' for those who used the company's Blogger product. In 2024, many blogs are hosted on either Blogger or WordPress. There are no rules around the structure or length of blogs, or any recommended frequency of update.

Microblogs

While YouTube and Facebook remain two of the most heavily used social networks in the social media sphere, in its day Twitter (now known as X) was the premier 'microblogging' site. In the early days, 'microblogs' were called 'tumblelogs', a term coined in 2005 (Viewsourcecode, 2025). Manton Reece, who founded the microblogging and social networking service Micro.blog, outlined the features that a microblog post should have.

Brevity was the order of the day, with messages lasting 280 characters at most, which is the upper limit for posts on X (formerly Twitter), once known as tweets. The earlier limit was 140 characters. By around 2006, the term microblog was used to apply to posts on both the Twitter and Tumblr platforms.

Other types of social media sites

Other types of social media site include idea-sharing boards like Pinterest; blogging and publishing networks like Medium and WordPress; product review sites like Trustpilot; company and organisation review sites like Glassdoor and Indeed; and vacation, accommodation and tourist attraction sites like TripAdvisor; and book suggestion websites like Goodreads.

Instagram, with its options for sharing photographs and stories 'on the spot', with stories designed to rapidly disappear, has two billion active users as of early 2024 (Dixon, 2024). Over 360 million of those users are located in India.

While YouTube may not seem a particularly obvious contender for a social media site that could be used in healthcare information, it is the second most popular site in this category in the world at the time of writing. It has over 2.7 billion active users per month (Global Media Insight, 2024).

More specialised social networking environments include the relatively corporate LinkedIn, a kind of 'professional Facebook'. There are also some specialised sites like NHS Futures and other organisationally hosted communities of practice offering as secure an environment as possible with current technology.

Other types of social media sites include virtual 3D worlds or 'metaverses' like Second Life and Meta, as well as online community and discussion sites like Digg, Quora and Reddit. Meta and Reddit in particular have attracted their fair share of controversy, which is considered in the later chapter on ethical aspects of using social media.

The uses of social media

Social media platforms like Facebook, X (Twitter), Instagram, WhatsApp, YouTube, TikTok and others are used not only for socialisation purposes, but for learning, knowledge acquisition, entertainment and keeping abreast of political and global events.

In terms of technological knowledge, SM users fall into two categories for Prensky (2001): digital natives and digital immigrants, although not all researchers agree. ('Digital natives' are usually deemed to be those born after 1980, who have never really known a world without the internet. This particularly applies to Generation Z.) This difference is partly due to the fact that with practice, anyone can gain basic digital skills. Digital 'immigrants' can, with practice and exposure, become as fluent as digital natives. This model also does not take into account aspects of what can be called the digital divide; a Millennial, for instance, who lacks access to online technology is not a digital native. Nor does this model take into account personal differences and preferences between individuals.

Case study: the lost land of GeoCities

Nothing lasts forever, as the saying goes and internet sites are no exception, no matter how robust they may seem at the time. Whether the terms used to describe the platforms are Web 2.0, social networking, or social media, platforms come and go.

In the decades since social media has been a part of our online lives, hundreds if not thousands of platforms have come and gone. Some of the best known include:

- Bebo
- Friends Reunited
- Friendster
- GeoCities
- MySpace
- SixDegrees.

GeoCities was an example of an early internet phenomenon, a kind of combined online social network all of its own. This web hosting service was launched in 1994, allowing users to create their own websites. The platform was organised into 'neighbourhoods', which were themed areas grouped by content. These neighbourhoods had names like 'Hollywood' for entertainment-related sites, 'SiliconValley' for technology-focused pages and 'Broadway' for more theatre- and arts-focused content. The health and fitness area was 'HotSprings' and several archived sites can still be seen at https://geocities.restorativland.org/HotSprings.

Founded by David Bohnett and John Rezner, GeoCities provided a platform where users were able to build personal and hobbyist websites free of charge. The service grew rapidly and before long it had become one of the most visited sites on the whole internet. In those early days of the web, the ethos of building websites was relatively home-spun philosophy. This was reflected in the design of GeoCities as a shared community. Web users shared ideas freely, including their knowledge and personal creations, with the platform allowing authors to incorporate images, video, sound clips and of course text into their pages.

GeoCities had a user-friendly interface that meant even those with limited technical skills were easily able to put their own web presence together. This early example of an online community had a vibrant and fresh community atmosphere. When Yahoo! acquired GeoCities in 1999 for approximately $3.57 billion, however, rival social media platforms were already on the rise, offering serious alternatives.

The popularity of GeoCities declined dramatically and the US version of GeoCities was closed down in 2009. It continued, however, to be operational in Japan for ten years after the US closure. Other sites filled the gap that GeoCities had occupied, with partial replacements including Facebook, Instagram, YouTube and Twitter (X) and, more recently sites like Digg, Reddit, Quora and various forums around the web.

Librarians and the adoption of social media

For many information professionals, new technology is extremely alluring. Many information professionals are by nature innovative and often technologically advanced, resulting in practitioners regularly having to acquire new knowledge and skills, particularly those of a technical nature. Librarians have had to gain awareness of, and skills in, using social media extremely rapidly. A Taylor & Francis survey in 2014 found that even at that relatively early point, over 70% of librarians were already using social media (Taylor & Francis Librarian Resources, 2014) .

Where circumstances have allowed, healthcare information professionals have frequently been amongst the most enthusiastic early adopters of new technologies. Examples have included 'virtual world' Second Life (Boulos, Hetherington and Wheeler, 2007), mobile technology (Chamberlain, Elcock and Puligari, 2015) and, more recently, artificial intelligence including large-language models (LLMs) such as ChatGPT (Zhang, 2023).

Many librarians have been quick to innovate and move to incorporate new technology into their workstreams and services to be able to provide users with more responsive services. Assuming an early adopter stance does not, however, always prove to be the long-term 'best option' for new technologies. Where staff power, funding and other resources are in short supply, it can be difficult to carve out the time needed to acquire new technical knowledge without neglecting existing core activities. In healthcare and academic libraries in particular, however, 'early adoption' of technologies frequently occurs as a direct response to queries from patrons or users. This early adoption can end up as an attempt to 'keep up' in a world where technological change is overwhelming and exponential.

Anderson (2007) has outlined several highly used key Web 2.0 applications and approaches, regardless of sector, including:

- blogging and microblogging
- podcasting and vodcasting
- RSS feeds
- social bookmarking and citation sharing
- social networking sites
- virtual worlds
- wikis.

In the next chapter, the focus is on some of the more specific applications of social media in healthcare and healthcare information settings.

CHAPTER 3

Social Media in Healthcare Settings

What is healthcare information?

Before we move on to look at the uses of social media in healthcare information, it's appropriate to consider the nature of healthcare information.

Although it's a somewhat broad classification, those who use health information can be divided into two main groups. One group delivers the care, or supports the delivery of care, while the second group encompasses those who receive care. Healthcare professionals and healthcare information professionals usually fall into the first group, while patients, residents, service users and the general public fall into the second – although of course users may fall into both groups at once.

The first group can be further subdivided into more defined professional groups, with each group requiring slightly different types of information. Registered medics, nurses and allied health professionals may need information to assist in patient treatment, enhance continuing professional development, or to gather evidence to support presentations, unit meetings, training or papers to present to organisational executives or board members. Students, on the other hand, may require simply a brief overview of conditions or interventions to support an assignment. And members of the public might require in-depth information about their condition or that of a loved one or dependant, or reassurance from others in a community with the same condition.

Whenever any new technology makes an appearance, there is often, understandably, scepticism over what is not yet tried and tested. In a world where being able to demonstrate the impact of everything we do is increasingly important to ensure our survival, it was apparent right from the start that an evidence base was required if the success of Library 2.0 or Web 2.0 initiatives were to be measured. Boxen (2008) was just one of those who noticed a lack of qualitative data in the literature that could help to combat this scepticism.

Library 2.0 was a term coined by Michael Casey, whose work highlights the focus on the user in the 2.0 world (Casey and Savastinuk, 2006). Regardless of whether the 2.0 label is applied to healthcare, libraries, or medicine, the features typically include:

- multimedia
- extensive use of networks that allow interaction with others
- personalised content
- a healthy attitude to scepticism around the content and source of the content.

Web 2.0 and Health Librarian 2.0

We have already seen how, from the start, healthcare librarians were actively involved in implementing the Web 2.0 technologies that underpin what we now call social media. From an early stage, this allowed the profession to both enhance the services they were able to offer in their libraries and to engage with service users. Gardois et al. (2012) identified the most frequently used technologies, which, in the early years, were wikis, blogs, social networking platforms and also instant messaging. Following the introduction of these technologies, communication with both professional clinicians and medical students was found to improve (Barsky and Giustini, 2007).

Along with the new terms Web 2.0, Library 2.0 and Librarian 2.0, Health Librarian 2.0 is another term that was coined as the new technologies began to be absorbed into everyday practice. Health Librarian 2.0 encompasses peer-to-peer online activity of medical professionals, e-learning, online medical publications and electronic health records. Another term that is sometimes used in connection with Health Librarian 2.0 is e-Patients, where patients may find out about new treatments or research due to their peer-to-peer online communication.

Healthcare information professionals have been at the forefront of using the internet, Web 2.0 and subsequently social media from the early years. Alongside the term 'Web 2.0' the term 'Library 2.0' emerged. This term encompassed the efforts that librarians made to both envisage and adopt the changes required in their attitudes and technological skills to engage effectively with users of social media. Once that knowledge had been acquired, it was not long before academic and medical libraries began offering advice and guidance to library users in the use of social media. At around the same time, Web 2.0 channels were pressed into service to promote library activity, incorporating blogs, wikis and online social networks.

The body of research contributed to the literature by healthcare librarians increased steadily, with a focus on describing social media and outlining the challenges of the then new Web 2.0 era for libraries. We saw earlier that terminology incorporated 'Web 2.0', 'Library 2.0' and 'Health 2.0' from a relatively early point. Alongside these terms, we can also contemplate 'Librarian 2.0' as it applies to healthcare information professionals in particular.

Despite the pervasiveness of social media in today's society in general and healthcare in particular, surprisingly little research appears to have been carried out into the use of social media in general in smaller libraries in the UK (Humphreys, 2019). This is a category into which many hospital and specialist services would fall, along with many academic healthcare or medical libraries. Even larger medical libraries attached to major universities usually have fewer than 20 staff, with many running on a staff of five or fewer.

Where do healthcare information professionals work?

Healthcare information professionals are known by many different titles: librarian; clinical librarian; information scientist; outreach librarian; healthcare information specialist; knowledge specialist; embedded librarian; and so many more. They work in a huge variety of settings: hospitals (acute, mental health and tertiary or specialist); universities and other places of education; research units; the corporate sector; policy units; government departments; pharmaceutical companies and other specialised organisations.

Healthcare information professionals work in a wide range of settings, from small specialised NHS libraries to large NHS Trusts and universities, research units, local and national government departments and private corporations. Other settings may include the uniformed armed services and health insurance companies. A small number of healthcare information professionals also work directly with patients or service users. There are relatively few posts of this kind in hospital settings, however, although some charities and non-profits may employ information officers, who often have responsibility for information placed on the web. In recent years, some public libraries also have librarians with special responsibilities for health information. Cross-sectoral partnership working is increasingly common (Hurt and Grundy, 2024; Evenstad, 2024).

Staffing levels in individual healthcare services are typically low, ranging from singleton librarians in smaller services to numbers in the low teens or, in some of the more fortunate larger services, in the low twenties. Kim (2023) has identified significant drops in numbers of librarians, along with archivists and curators, in academic services alone. Hospital library staffing levels dropped substantially in the early 1990s and the early 2020s; the pattern continues (De-la-Mano, 2024). De-la-Mano also highlights the expanding roles that many health librarians play in the areas of research, education and critical appraisal of evidence.

Professional roles vary, from the traditional concept of a librarian or library manager to clinical librarians, outreach librarians and, in some cases, specialist trainers or systems and electronic resources librarians. In the NHS and university settings, typically the role will involve some traditional work areas like selection of resources, cataloguing and classification. The majority of work, however, includes analysing, selecting and collating information for literature searching and current awareness, as well as educating users and promoting and advocating for the service, increasingly necessary in a world where severe cuts happen regularly.

The adoption of social media by healthcare librarians

Librarians are, in general, curious individuals. Many love a good puzzle and derive great satisfaction from acquiring new skills to help our users and, often, simply for the sake of acquiring fresh knowledge. Medicine and healthcare are areas that are constantly changing, as new discoveries are found almost on a daily basis and typically, our users expect us to keep abreast of these developments. The requirement to constantly acquire these new skills, however, means that we need to constantly keep abreast of changes in technology, even where we might not have the opportunity for formal training in the ever-changing skills and responsibilities expected of the profession.

Along the way, healthcare librarians have had to constantly acquire new skills so that they can make effective use of social media – what Chewe, Sakala and Zulu (2021) call 'social media literacy skills'. This skills acquisition has not always come easily, however, with lack of training opportunities just one of the identified barriers to overcome.

Despite the potential benefits of social media, it was not always a given in the early days that healthcare librarians would adopt these apps and approaches in their practice. On occasions, healthcare information professionals appeared to have settled for what Giustini (2010) described as 'quiet acceptance'. It is interesting that Giustini also identified both Twitter and the virtual world Second Life as 'peripheral' at this point, a prediction which has proved to be only partially accurate in the case of Twitter (X), with the benefit of hindsight.

Social media and the role of healthcare information professionals

Since the early days of Web 2.0 and social media, some medical professionals have expressed concern about the quality of health information on the internet (Scullard, Peacock and Davies, 2010) and Web 2.0 sites especially (Dalmer, 2017). Some other authors, however, regard the best Web 2.0 sites as valid sources of information (Laurent and Vickers, 2009). One of the main functions of information professionals in the healthcare field is to ensure that healthcare professionals can access authoritative information. We also need to ensure users have the critical appraisal skills and tools to decide if the information is authoritative.

The rise of social media use in healthcare information

Social media applications are now incorporated into several aspects of healthcare information provision. These include but are not limited to: CPD, education, engaging with users, information literacy, journal clubs, knowledge management, online collaboration and patient and consumer support.

Fernández-Luque and Bau (2015) highlighted how, even in the mid-2010s, social media use was on the rise. Their research showed that, although there were some regional variations, the top three social media applications remained consistent, if not always in the same order of popularity, in South Korea, Nigeria, the USA and the UK. As often happens, the UK trailed the USA in terms of uptake of this new technology in hospital settings, although in European terms the UK and the Netherlands led the field.

In the previous chapter we looked at some of the general uses of social media. One of the joys of social media is that it can easily be adapted and specialised for particular sectors. When it comes to healthcare information, social media platforms are also one of the fastest modes of public health awareness. Some of this information can be retrieved via a straightforward 'vanilla' web search, but there are other methods of tracking down information on social media that are unique to this way of communicating.

The most common areas for social media in healthcare

For those who work in healthcare environments, particularly where they are dealing directly with patients, it's vital that clinicians have access to the most up-to-date evidence-based information possible. In addition, many clinicians are extremely time-poor, making it very challenging for them to access evidence-based resources to support their practice (Haynes and Haines, 1998).

As we have seen, social media network sites are online platforms through which individuals, groups and organisations create presence and share information through texts, photos, music videos and other multimedia content. Since the earliest stages of its development, social media has been a natural tool for use in medical and healthcare settings. Typical uses include 'patient communication, professional development and knowledge-sharing opportunities' (Jeyaraman et al., 2023).

Some of the most common areas for social media to be utilised in healthcare are in health promotion, including public health messaging; research; marketing and/or branding for both individuals and organisations (including hospitals); and recruitment (Farsi, 2021). Social media has altered the relationships between patients and clinicians due to the better overall understanding of health information (Farsi, 2021). As we will see in the chapter on ethics, however, this can be something of a double-edged sword.

Many healthcare professionals now use social media to educate patients and the general public, either as a representative of their organisation, or as an individual, operating within their ethical professional frameworks. Just some of the topics where social media has been used to communicate with and educate patients include drugs, eating disorders, smoking cessation, vaccines and, of course, pandemics. Social media also offers an opportunity for continuing professional development (CPD) for both healthcare information professionals and for clinicians, as well as a potential networking tool.

Healthcare information wikis

Wikis are another area of social media that can offer a wealth of information at low cost – providing the information is peer-reviewed regularly. Wikis are collaborative online knowledge bases, held on a website, that anyone can edit. Users are able to create, modify and link pages linked to specific topics or subjects. Many wikis become a kind of digital encyclopaedia that is, ideally, constantly being updated by the community using it.

There are a couple of rumours surrounding the origin of the word wiki, with one theory stating it stands for 'what I know is' and the other claiming it derives from the Hawaiian phrase 'wiki wiki', which means fast or speedy. So the story goes, the name was chosen by Ward Cunningham, creator of the original wiki, as he wanted to emphasise the rapid and collaborative nature of the platform.

Wikipedia is probably the best known wiki of our time, but there are several specialised healthcare-related wikis including WikiDoc, which uses the strapline 'The Living Textbook of Medicine' for general medicine. Although the wiki still exists, several entries have not been updated for some time, therefore requiring users to proceed with caution – a common theme when it comes to using social media as an information source.

Radiopaedia fares somewhat better, with tiered membership models including free access for over 125 low- and middle-income countries. The focus, as the title suggested, is on medical imaging and entries list the date when the article or post was last updated. Others include WikiAnesthesia for those in anaesthetics; WikEM for 'global emergency medicine' and WikiMSK, primarily aimed at those in musculoskeletal medicine in New Zealand.

Fandom wikis are also common, for example there are Wikis for *New Amsterdam*, *Holby*, covering the fictional hospital that provides the setting for the BBC TV world of *Casualty* and *Holby City*, and *Scrubs*. Readers can see when a page was last updated, although in common with all internet pages, caution should be applied, as edits may refer only to the correction of a typo rather than a full review of the content.

Multiple users can contribute to the content of many wikis, sometimes simultaneously. Like GeoCities, the interface is typically simple, with no special technical skills required. One feature of wikis that is not always present in other social media platforms, however, is the inbuilt version control. Since changes are tracked, it's easy to roll back a site to a previous version if required – a potentially invaluable tool in the case of misinformation.

Mobile devices in healthcare information

In settings where access to desktop computers is limited, mobile devices and apps can be a useful tool to overcome this. The use of these devices has been shown to result in improved clinical decision-making and better patient outcomes (Ventola, 2014b). Mobile technology and social media would appear to be something of a match made in heaven. Authors have identified eight key themes that can, however, affect clinicians' take-up of mobile technology: 'usefulness, ease of use, design, compatibility, technical issues, content, personalization and convenience' (Jacob, Sanchez-Vazquez and Ivory, 2020).

Although the smartphone (or iPhone for Apple aficionados) now dominates, over the years there have been various experiments with mobile technologies and terminologies. These studies have included several studies of the effectiveness of using Personal Digital Assistants (PDAs) (Morgen, 2003; Garritty and El Emam, 2006). In the subsequent decade, ownership of PDAs amongst certain groups of clinicians increased (Divall, Camosso-Stefinovic and Baker, 2013). PDAs were even sometimes described as offering a 'walking library' in the early to mid-2000s (Wiggins, 2004).

How trustworthy *is* online healthcare information?

As we'll see in a later chapter and as has already been highlighted in the specific case of wikis, one of the difficulties with online healthcare information in general is whether or not it can be trusted. This includes both the currency of the information and how recently it has been checked by a subject-matter expert.

This is an area where librarians and healthcare information professionals can offer their services with confidence, not necessarily in checking the information themselves, but in assessing the trustworthiness of the information and in signposting to experts. One significant and specific role for healthcare information professionals in this area lies in helping users to critically appraise content and identify conflicts of interest that may not always be apparent, as well as checking both content and credentials of those who have contributed posts.

Incorporating social media into workflows

In the early days, many libraries made use of some very specific Web 2.0 technologies to offer websites to their users. Although most of the free sites have long since been superseded, other platforms and apps included Netvibes and Pageflakes (McCormick and Pickard, 2013); Yahoo Pipes (Tattersall, Beecroft and Cantrell, 2011); and Pinterest (Parvin, 2018). These allowed for relatively easy content aggregation, the use of RSS readers without any additional software required and curation tools.

When it comes to designing social media sites, there is research that can help librarians give their sites the maximum chance of allowing users to engage. Syn (2023) has highlighted, for instance, that Facebook users like to check the identity of the health information provider via the banner, while images in particular draw and hold attention.

Time pressures remain a major factor, with several users requiring assistance with research, data management and metrics relating to publication. In a question and answer session at the Medical Library Association's 2018 summit, the impact of Superstorm Sandy in 2012 arose: this weather event destroyed the NYU Health Sciences Library. NYU Library Director, Jeff D. Williams explained how, with no physical library to offer an anchor, the only option was to come up with different ways of working. The need to use appropriate semantics was also highlighted, as well as the possibility of anticipating future changes that might influence decisions in healthcare.

As became very clear during the COVID-19 pandemic, social media can have a very powerful impact on health decisions. Librarians are well placed to use content analysis, sentiment analysis and other text-mining techniques to help health practitioners gain a better understanding of social media and how it could be used to help with decision-making at global as well as local, national or corporate level (Fernández-Luque and Bau, 2015).

While there may be concerns about some aspects of social media from an ethical perspective, an area which will be covered in a later chapter, many posts, tweets and other social media outputs are easily viewable in the public domain.

How healthcare librarians use social media

Since social media first became a 'big thing' in around 2010, healthcare librarians have engaged in a wide range of projects. Typically, they have used social media to enhance services and engage with communities, market and promote services, signpost users to information, reach out to users and find cost-effective methods of professional development amongst others (Jeyaraman et al., 2023).

Healthcare information professionals have also assisted users to overcome barriers in implementing social media, including identifying privacy issues (Elliott, 2014) and, especially in the early days, assisting with the learning curves of using social media (Joo, Choi and Baek, 2018). These learning curves can be steeper than is often recognised. Once it was no longer primarily the domain of defence and became widespread throughout research and academia, academic librarians were amongst the first groups to establish themselves and their organisations on social media (Collins and Quan-Haase, 2012).

In the days of Web 2.0, before social media was quite as widespread as it is now, it offered healthcare libraries an alternative to official web pages, with Netvibes and Pageflakes in particular offering a chance to circumnavigate the often draconian barriers to making users aware of what the service had to offer. James Cook University Hospital, for example, used their Netvibes start-up page as a portal for current awareness (McCormick and Pickard, 2013). Social media also offers the opportunity for healthcare information professionals to incorporate and spread the word about innovations. One of the advantages of many social media sites lies in the fact that once they're established, social media pages are relatively easy to maintain. Blogs, social bookmarking and social networking sites were amongst the early techniques used to reach out to their users (Zohoorian-Fooladi and Abrizah, 2013) and in some cases are still in use today. Social tags in folksonomies are, however, far from a perfect method of classifying data, although they can be particularly useful for smaller collections of documents and management of citations.

Social media can also offer healthcare librarians a cost-effective and inclusive outreach option. In some cases, it allows healthcare information professionals to successfully reach users who might otherwise be excluded or find it difficult to use library services and in more distant locations.

Healthcare librarians have been utilising social media platforms to engage with users and disseminate health information almost since they appeared on the scene. Twitter (X), in particular, has emerged as a valuable tool for health libraries to reach their audience, promote services and respond to user queries (Waddell, Barnes and Khan-Kernahan, 2012).

Social media can offer a cost-effective way for librarians to communicate with peers and to widen the circle of practice, as well as offer a convenient way to communicate with users. Just some of the ways in which librarians in healthcare settings have used and still use, social media include:

- career development and networking
- creating YouTube channels
- contribution to health literacy and other health campaigns
- curation of information
- current awareness
- dissemination of papers published by researchers attached to organisations
- Facebook and/or Instagram, for promotion and for holding online teaching sessions
- helping to recruit candidates for research projects
- journal clubs
- promotion of the service (Omini and Osuolale, 2019)
- Twitter (X) for promotion – with one particularly notable campaign, A Million Decisions, rolled out nationally to highlight the vast number of decisions made daily in healthcare, from patient care to policy implementation to resource allocation and the role played by librarians and knowledge specialists in ensuring the decisions were backed up with evidence-based papers and research
- Wikis.

Social media in healthcare information: benefits and risks

Social media can benefit healthcare organisations, clinicians and patients in various ways, including community engagement, networking, education and patient support (Househ, 2013). However, the use of social media in healthcare also presents potential risks, such as privacy violations and unreliable information (Ventola, 2014a). To maximise the impact of social media strategies, healthcare librarians should develop goal-oriented approaches with measurable metrics for success (Waddell, Barnes and Khan-Kernahan, 2012). While some healthcare administrators may be hesitant about social media use in the workplace, it can be a valuable asset for modern, well-run healthcare institutions when used wisely (Leman, 2012).

The risks of data ending up in regimes not as tightly controlled as the European Union (EU) or the UK are real. As cyberhackers have become more and more sophisticated, additional security has been added out of necessity. It's often no longer enough to simply have usernames and passwords. We now often require Multi Factor Authentication (MFA) via a code generated by a mobile phone or e-mail account and even, in some cases, biometric data such as a fingerprint or even face recognition – once the preserve of science fiction novelists.

Patients, patient data and social media

In many if not most healthcare settings, librarians are concerned with never losing sight of the fact that everything, ultimately, is to help clinical and healthcare colleagues to improve patient care.

In health information settings, it has become increasingly important to recognise and understand user interactions and expectations with regards to social media. Research suggests that more and more patients have already begun to rely on online resources to receive health information. In response, many health organisations have turned to social media and microblogging services to try and meet those needs. The ease of posting and sharing information on Twitter (X) makes it an essential tool for health libraries to reach their users.

Social media platforms commonly used in healthcare

Since the arrival of social media in our worlds, it has become a powerful tool in healthcare, allowing healthcare professionals to reach out to and engage with patients, raise awareness around health issues and build trust in both organisations and individuals.

Facebook

Although some sources believe that Facebook's star is on the wane, it remains the most popular platform globally. For healthcare libraries, it has often offered a platform that allows interaction with library users, students and healthcare professionals on a relatively personal level. Typically, uses have included employing Facebook as a kind of home page for the service, with details of staffed opening hours and events. Other uses have included the promotion of books, articles and academic papers. However, as we will see later, in the chapter on ethical and moral considerations, Facebook is not without its controversies, particularly the handling of personal data. The connection with Cambridge Analytica in particular damaged the brand, leading to high levels of distrust (McCallum, 2022).

Twitter (X)

X (formerly Twitter) was the dominant platform for microblogging and instant comments, at least until it was purchased by multi-billionaire Elon Musk in 2022. The number of monthly active users is now estimated at around 368 million, with the USA accounting for the largest percentage, at 95.4 million users. On average, active users worldwide spend around 3.49 hours per day on their mobile phones (Petrosyan, 2024). In its heyday, Twitter described itself as 'what's happening in the world and what people are talking about right now' (Twitter, 2020). Users may post, access and forward short 'tweets', pithy text messages, images or video posts.

Originally tweets were limited to 140 characters, although the limit was increased in 2018 to 240 characters. The number of followers an account has is one measure of success, with the more followers the better, and the level of engagement for a post can often be seen from the number of comments.

In 2023, after Elon Musk bought Twitter, some of the charming and immediately recognisable features, such as the small blue bird, disappeared and X was born. There have been attempts by rivals to create alternatives, but at the time of writing neither Facebook's Threads, independently run Mastodon, nor any of the others have gained the kind of social traction that Twitter once enjoyed. This includes the Truth Social network promoted by the 45th President of the United States (Wikipedia, 2025).

The Twitter microblogging platform allows its users to post and access short posts incorporating text, image, audio or video, often referred to as tweets, in line with the bird-like branding. In 2018 the sharing of both website links and multimedia content was allowed. Since the early years, users have acquired followers, either organically or by buying them (Stringhini et al., 2013).

YouTube

YouTube, the pre-eminent site globally for sharing video content, has a name that is derivative and clear once you understand the origin of the words. The

You makes it apparent that the content is user-generated – even where the user is, for example, a major movie studio. The Tube derives from an old name for television, when screens did not rely on liquid crystal display (LCD) or plasma, but cathode-ray tubes (CRTs).

LinkedIn

Although it may appear independent on the surface, the highly popular professional social media site LinkedIn has been owned by Microsoft since 2016. Although users can create and share posts and upload content, they are mainly business-oriented in character. The site is mostly used for networking between professionals, job openings and signalling that users are open to new opportunities.

It can also be an invaluable source of information to help healthcare professionals make links between researchers and, in some cases, even contact researchers directly for clarification on research carried out. LinkedIn was launched in 2003 and like many of the 'dot.com' companies, it originated in the living room of one of its founders.

TikTok

TikTok, one of the most recent platforms to emerge, is on the ascendant and has become known as a platform for dancing, lip-synching and conversational/review purposes (Ostrovsky and Chen, 2020). One of the unique aspects of TikTok is the 'For You' page, where most of the viewed content is selected randomly. As a result, TikTok generates an audience that is wider and more diverse than the traditional social media model, which was based on 'followers'.

Although TikTok in general is associated with younger internet users, as has been the case with FriendsReunited, Facebook, Twitter (X) and many more, the platform has gradually made its way into the lives of older adults (Ng and Indran, 2023). As they noted in their thematic analysis of the way in which older adults (defined as over 60) use the platform, this included a large percentage of videos 'defying age stereotypes' as well as 'making light of age-related vulnerabilities' and 'calling out ageism'.

Healthcare professionals have also used TikTok, described as a 'short-form video social media platform', to share information including insights into their professions and their scope of practice. One of the issues is the lack of evidence that investigates how some professions are utilising the platform, including occupational therapists. Methods that can be used for this purpose include content analysis and sentiment analysis. Chasca et al. (2023) have identified the potential for building communities of practice, collaborating over innovations and sharing information. They have also highlighted the need for future research to monitor the quality of the information on the platform and counter inaccuracies.

The most appropriate (social media) tool for the job

Choosing the most appropriate platforms to reach members of the target audience is vital to their success. Facebook, Instagram and X, for example, may be the most suitable for visuals, with TikTok currently the forerunner for short film clips. LinkedIn, on the other hand, is better for professional networking and mainly text-based, with occasional visual images or short clips in support. It's worth noting that LinkedIn is unblocked even in many NHS organisations, possibly due to its perceived position as arguably the pre-eminent business social network, without the distractions of cat videos, advertisements and other consumer content commonly found on Facebook and other more general platforms.

Healthcare librarians can leverage social media through regular posts that maintain audience interest and engagement, monitoring the performance of what does and doesn't work by assessing monitoring and analytics. Collaboration between organisations can also offer a time-effective and co-ordinated partnership approach to using social media.

Popularity of platforms

Despite a relative lack of coverage in the professional information management literature (Hendrix et al., 2009), experience and anecdotal evidence shows that social media platforms have a range of uses in healthcare science libraries.

These uses range from informal web pages and maintaining a presence on the internet for marketing and outreach purposes (Garcia-Milian, Norton and Tennant, 2012). When Kordzadeh and Young (2018) analysed three months' worth of 1,700 Facebook posts made by 17 hospitals in the USA, they found that major themes included the provision of health information, recognising special celebration days and employee recognition. Later research by Mohammadi et al. (2018) showed that, although health is a popular topic on Facebook, certain health and biomedical topics attract more attention than others, namely general and internal medicine as well as complementary and alternative medicine.

Twitter, in its early days, was another favourite, used extensively for outreach (Cuddy, Graham and Morton-Owens, 2010) as well as informing followers. A content analysis of 524 tweets from four one-week periods in 2014 revealed that Twitter was being used mainly as a tool for current awareness (Neilson, 2016).

Blogging was another popular Web 2.0/social media platform used in many libraries, offering a prompt, fresh and convenient way to keep library patrons apprised of events and activity (Sapp and Cogdill, 2010). Akers (2019) has explored how Jeff D. Williams of New York University has outlined how librarians have adapted services to respond to the changing needs of users, inviting healthcare information professionals to take something of a longitudinal view. Following the focus group work, it became apparent that the users typically encountered today are both more experienced and comfortable with technology but are, however, less patient when access systems are complex.

Successful social media campaigns in healthcare

Some of the most successful social media campaigns in healthcare have included Stoptober, a UK government-led, behaviour theory-supported programme to encourage smoking cessation in the population. Others were British Foundation Resuscitation campaigns; 'This Girl Can' from Sport England, to encourage participation in sport; and various public health campaigns around food, including '5 A Day' to encourage healthy eating. Social media is now used as one of the foremost channels to raise awareness on health days around the world. As well as those already mentioned, social media is often used to raise awareness in particular where distinct communities or demographics are involved. These include Macmillan Cancer's World's Biggest Coffee Morning and Movember, which draws attention to men's health issues, such as prostate cancer, testicular cancer and men's suicide.

The most successful social media campaigns around particular conditions share genuine stories of those with personal experience – experts by experience, as the phrase goes. Sharing positive patient experiences of overcoming challenges related to their conditions, or supporting others to do so, is generally thought to result in high levels of engagement. This approach offers inspiration to others and the chance for the organisation to build and maintain credibility.

Once the credibility is established, providing accurate health information can position the organisation as a trusted source for social media users. A social media presence can lead casual users to principal websites via leading hyperlinks or multimedia. Although the Health on the Net Foundation code of conduct (HONcode) is sadly no longer extant following the demise of the organisation, in the UK the Patient Information Forum (PIF) standard is one way for patients and the general public to be reassured that the site you visit is evidence-based, easy to access and has been put together by those with in-depth knowledge and experience of the topic. Using images, videos, voice recordings and even interactive elements, can also capture the attention of users as well as conveying information effectively and economically.

Social media also offers the opportunity for engagement throughout a community, encouraging participants in the community to interact, share conversations and show their engagement levels through comments, likes and shares. Social media posts often incorporate a clear 'call to action', as marketing experts call it. Audience members are guided towards desired actions, which may be donating time or money, scheduling appointments, or simply sharing the post.

Demonstrating impact

Healthcare libraries are often constrained by budgets, staff, environments or organisational support, or all of these, and managers in particular are often called on to demonstrate how their work impacts the organisation's corporate goals.

However, libraries that lack systematic metrics for measuring success can find themselves pouring precious resources into social media upkeep without knowing if they are promoting their strategic vision. Healthcare librarians can, of course, simply use Twitter (X) and other social media platforms as a marketing and promotion tool, but one way to measure impact is to assess how engaged their communities are. Librarians can use the two-way communication and instant feedback that social media makes possible to develop services that are more customer-focused and user-friendly and make the user feel they are being heard.

In addition, this results in more accurate metrics to demonstrate what approaches are working well and which strategies have been less successful. In turn, these strategies can feed into organisational strategic goals.

Above all, social media offers a way to communicate. Indeed, for Thielst (2010), three of the major ways that social media can be used by healthcare librarians can be summarised as 'Connect, Communicate, Collaborate'.

Demographic preferences of social media use and the implications for librarians

Social media and the internet in general were, certainly in the early days of their development, mostly aimed at the younger generation. By 2014, just under half of those between 18 and 29 in a serious relationship agreed that the internet had had an impact on their relationships and the number of estimated internet users that year was 3 billion – or just under half the then world population of 7.2 billion.

While, in the west, Facebook and Twitter (X) remain two of the most popular platforms, that isn't the case in some other parts of the world. In China, for instance, Weibo and WeChat are the most popular platforms. This is likely to be due, at least in part, to apps such as WhatsApp being blocked (Guyoncourt, 2024a).

When deciding what social media platform to use, it can be especially helpful to take demographics into account. Some social media platforms are more popular with those born within a particular 'generation', or a particular geography.

Although social media platforms can differ in the demographics of those who prefer to use them, there are some commonalities. The most popular social media platforms worldwide remain Facebook, YouTube, X (formerly Twitter) – although this platform has been losing ground since it was purchased by Elon Musk and rebranded – along with Instagram, TikTok and, from a professional perspective, LinkedIn. The Chinese social media platform, Weibo, often described as similar to Twitter (X) if not directly equivalent, has at least 480 million estimated users. WeChat, the Chinese equivalent of WhatsApp, has around 1.17 billion users.

Although it is, arguably, one of the most intergenerational platforms, Facebook is most popular with those between 18 and 44, with more males than females using the platform. (Herd Digital, 2022).

The user base of relative 'new kid on the social media block' TikTok has a younger demographic in general. Users are concentrated in the 18–34 age group, with a larger percentage of users identifying as male (Ceci, 2024).

Which gender?

Different social media platforms often differ in the demographics of those who use them, with Facebook appealing more to male users than female users and more commonly used in urban rather than suburban settings. Age-wise, those aged 18–29 years and 30–49 years are represented particularly well on Facebook.

Female users were also more likely to be found on Instagram, which had around one billion users around the world, with the highest percentage in the USA. The age range was mostly between 25 and 34 years.

The demographics of users of X (formerly Twitter)

While Facebook remains the dominant social platform around the world, at least for now, Twitter has also been extremely influential. It had over 330 million users in 2022 following its purchase by multi-billionaire Elon Musk. It was renamed X as of 2023, with the rebrand completed in 2024. Although Twitter was one of the top five social media platforms for several years, following the acquisition, the number of users on X had fallen by 23% by November of that year (Hern, 2024).

In some countries, X is not in use at all: in China, for instance, over 480 million users are on Weibo, which shares many similarities with Twitter. During the COVID-19 pandemic, it was apparent that Weibo fulfilled many of the same functions that Twitter did in the rest of the world. Elon Musk has made no secret of the fact that one of the drivers behind his purchase of Twitter is for it to become a global rival to the popular Chinese platform WeChat (Milmo and Hawkins, 2023).

In contrast to Facebook and Instagram, for Milmo and Hawkes Twitter appealed more to male users; the most frequent users were in the USA, Japan and India. The Twitter platform was, for many years, the social media platform of choice of the 45th President of the United States and was used as a frequent messaging channel during the COVID-19 pandemic.

Demographics of WhatsApp users

WhatsApp, the mobile messaging app with strong in-built levels of security, is another that is traditionally particularly appealing to a younger audience, with WeChat fulfilling this function in China. China has blocked WhatsApp and other foreign messaging apps due to its strict internet censorship policy. This policy, often referred to as the 'Great Firewall of China', aims to control the information flow within the country.

By restricting access to foreign platforms, the Chinese government can more effectively monitor and control the information its citizens consume and in addition, the bans in place encourage users to opt for Chinese-developed apps such as WeChat. These have greater capabilities for surveillance and tighter levels of control.

In 2014, secure chat messaging platform WhatsApp was purchased by Facebook for US$ 19 billion. Its popularity is also high, with 2 billion active users around the world. The average Android WhatsApp user spends just over 33 minutes per day on the app and the highest number of monthly active users are in India (487.5 million) (Dean, 2022).

Demographics of YouTube users

YouTube, the most popular sharing platform for music and film clips, is also found worldwide. There are exceptions, notably where it is blocked or censored in a territory. The majority of users are male rather than female, although it appears to be equally popular whether the setting is urban, suburban, or rural. YouTube allows users to create and share playlists, comment on clips (unless the originator has turned off commenting) and create their own channels. Some medical schools and many hospitals and healthcare organisations have a presence on YouTube, although, as we will see later in the chapter on barriers, that doesn't necessarily mean it's possible to access YouTube content from within healthcare settings.

There are other social media platforms that are less general in scope, such as LinkedIn. This platform in particular is mostly used for networking, sharing of posts and maintaining a professional profile. The site was launched in 2003 and Microsoft acquired LinkedIn in 2016.

The following chapters take a more in-depth look at some specific aspects of social media usage in healthcare information settings.

CHAPTER 4

Social Media in Healthcare Research

Introduction

One area of healthcare information where social media shows tremendous potential is that of research.

This may involve reaching out to potential subjects or research partners in the first place, 'horizon scanning' for emerging – or re-emerging – topics or, once the research or phase is complete, disseminating the results. It may also be a fruitful way of connecting researchers with further potential research partners and funding streams. According to Elliott (2014), social media can facilitate all of these. Other identified uses included the possibility of using social media to advance research careers and promote the reputation of a healthcare organisation as a leading research institute.

Using social media for healthcare research can however, be fraught with difficulties and controversies. These may include the difficulty of applying relatively formulaic medical research techniques and approaches to a system that is intrinsically informal.

Popularity of social media platforms for health research recruitment

Historically, Facebook was the most popular platform for recruitment of research participants, followed by Twitter, although the latter was some way behind. Despite some concern that Facebook has been losing market share and/or social reach, Bour et al. (2021) found that Facebook remained one of, if not the, leading social media platforms for health research. Although other platforms including YouTube, Instagram and LinkedIn were also mentioned, they appeared to be relatively infrequently used compared to the two market leaders. One of the key findings related to the ability of social media to recruit participants from populations which have traditionally been difficult to recruit. This may be due to factors such as mobility challenges, social disadvantage or low disease prevalence.

Bour et al. also acknowledge the way in which COVID-19 has changed the way in which social media was used to not only spread information but to 'share diagnostic, treatment and even follow-up protocols'. Not only that, it has also allowed users in healthcare 'to develop infoveillance studies to help characterise disease distribution and behaviours critical to the early stages of an outbreak . . . and to recruit participants in order to collect large-scale data within a short time period'. Bour et al. also highlighted the heterogeneity in the approaches used across platforms.

Topolovec-Vranic and Natarajan (2016) discovered that 40% of the studies they looked at described SM as the most effective method of recruitment, with 50% of the studies describing their target research population as hard to reach. The hashtag was thought to be an effective option for tailoring recruitment campaigns, particularly where they reflected the interests of the target research subjects.

Social exclusion and inequalities may play a part in the decision on user groups to target for research. Some of those with disabilities or at a social disadvantage, for example, may not have internet access. Those with home internet access may fall disproportionately into the middle class, as was demonstrated during COVID-19 lockdowns in the case of education (Cullinane and Montacute, 2020). Researchers must therefore make a decision about the appropriateness of using social media as the sole method of recruiting participants or whether it has the most merit as an additional method supporting more traditional methods of recruitment.

A contentious but valid aspect to consider when recruiting research participants via social media is that they may not be entirely representative of the overall population of interest to the research team. Researchers must also frequently be on the alert for fake participants (Peach et al., 2023). Notwithstanding this, one of the most positive aspects of social media is that it can easily be adapted and tweaked to personalise it for different audiences. It is likely that this will increase as artificial intelligence (AI) becomes a more salient feature of the research landscape.

In spite of these concerns and limitations, using social media as a channel for healthcare research recruitment can offer advantages such as expanded geographical reach, time savings and increased accessibility (Darko, Kleib and Olson, 2022; Jones, Wilson-Keates and Melrose, 2024). The use of social media to recruit, collate and disseminate results from research will probably continue to evolve.

Despite the potential pitfalls, social media offers a unique, real-time opportunity to garner insights into what people really think about healthcare interventions. Just some of the ways in which social media has been used in this area for research include 'recruitment, data mining, social media initiatives or campaigns, hashtag communities and journal clubs' (Dol et al., 2019). In the Dol study, participant recruitment was by far the most common use of social media. Other uses included conference tweeting, virtual journal clubs and, in a small number of cases, patient education and care.

Privacy of research subjects in social media

The need for using social media in research, as well as the requirement for ethical and professional guidelines, has been identified in several studies (Jeyaraman et al., 2023). While social media sites can be an effective and low-cost way for researchers hoping to reach their intended audience, caution is required to manage the risks around patient privacy and confidentiality. These areas will be explored in more detail in a later chapter on moral and ethical issues around social media in healthcare information.

One way of ensuring – or at least attempting to ensure – the quality of the insights uncovered and the research approach would be to use the CHEKC framework. This framework was introduced by Sohn et al. (2017). In this framework, the abbreviation stands for 'Crowdsourced Health Experience-ontologies-based healthcare Knowledge Creation'. The CHECKC framework provides patients with information about healthcare based on healthcare experiences, symptoms and conditions which are similar. Arguably, this makes the CHEKC framework a better choice, at least in terms of accuracy and efficiency, than the PatientsLikeMe (PLM) framework2 (Wicks et al., 2010).

Advantages and disadvantages of social media for recruiting healthcare research participants

Despite the concerns highlighted above, a further advantage of using social media to recruit participants lies in its cost-effectiveness (Walsh and Carter-Bawa, 2023). It can require effort to identify the most appropriate social media platform to reach the target group.

Perhaps paradoxically, social media apps also offer an opportunity to widen access to research. It offers a way of potentially reaching those who may be typically regarded as marginalised or difficult groups (Jones, Wilson-Keates and Melrose, 2024; Iflaifel et al., 2023). Social media also has the advantage of making it relatively easy for researchers to contact ordinary people who use the platforms, rather than confining their recruitment to what can sometimes feel like an academic research echo chamber.

For Denecke et al. (2018), one of the major risks is that research participants may self-select. Those with an interest in the area of study may be preferred for recruitment, resulting in a less representative research sample. Particular ethnicities may also be over-represented if social media is used as a recruitment method (Benedict et al., 2019). Paradoxically, however, in some cases recruiting via social media can mean that the recruitment net is cast wider (Langer et al., 2021).

Ensuring that research ideas are not compromised or stolen can also be a hazard of using social media for research, combined with the risk that research recruits may share information with others participating. Even where this is not intentional, the integrity of the study may be put at risk, meaning social media may not be the optimal method for recruiting to double blind trials, for example. Healthcare information professionals can help advise the research team about whether there are methods to overcome this. For Darko, Kleib and Olson (2022), input from ethics boards is another essential consideration to ensure optimum use in the area of recruitment in particular. Those working in public health research especially have a responsibility to ensure they have taken into account the impacts of, for example, TikTok on health, possibly advocating changes that may be needed (Zenone, Ow and Barbic, 2021).

Extracting and analysing data from social media healthcare research

Another area where healthcare information professionals can add value is in the area of assisting with the extraction and analysis of the results generated by healthcare research on social media. Ellis and Reichel (2023) identified text mining and topic modelling as two approaches that helped to make sense of a dataset of parasitology tweets from 2011 to 2020.

Topic modelling

Topic modelling can be defined as 'a type of statistical modelling that uses unsupervised Machine Learning to identify clusters or groups of similar words within a body of text' (Sheridan, 2022). The type of data extracted from social media may take the form of text, images, videos and audio, as well as metadata about time, location and engagement information relating to posts.

Two specific types of topic modelling are Latent Semantic Analysis (LSA) and Latent Dirichlet Allocation (LDA). The first uncovers hidden relationships between words in a text, assuming that words used in similar contexts have related meanings. LDA identifies topics and can analyse multiple documents simultaneously, helping with both classification and categorisation of text data based on the content.

D'Souza, Hooten and Murad (2021) also identified the need for extracting data in a systematic manner, ensuring that quality and potential bias were addressed, data was analysed and study findings interpreted appropriately. Zhou et al. (2018) add other aspects that need to be addressed with regards to the use of social media for research. These include ethics and governance, confidentiality and privacy, professionalism and quality of information, particularly where results and research apply to patients, one of the most delicate and sensitive aspects of using social media to assist with research.

Other options for extracting the data may include web scraping, where data is extracted directly from web pages, including text, images and links. This does, however, require a relatively high level of programming ability and is also likely to require a serious time investment. While commercial tools are available, the cost is often prohibitive for most healthcare libraries and information units.

Content analysis, sentiment analysis and network analysis

The content analysis method is used to systematically analyse and interpret qualitative data, from books, articles, speeches and social media posts, or from audio or video files or even from photographs or paintings. The aim is to identify patterns, themes or meanings in the data and coding systems can be used to categorise and quantify the data, meaning statistical analysis can also be carried out.

Sentiment analysis is a technique used to determine the emotional tone behind a piece of text. If you break it down, it's an attempt to teach computers to understand and classify human sentiments, with the most basic approach to categorise text as positive, negative, or neutral. Some advanced techniques in this approach are more sophisticated, capable of identifying specific emotions like anger or sadness, joy or fear. Sentiment analysis is particularly useful for businesses and organisations to understand public opinion and was used during the COVID-19 pandemic.

Network analysis is a technique used to study the relationships between entities or elements in a network, represented by nodes. These entities might be people or organisations, or anything else connected by some kind of relationship. Social networks encompass people and their relationships with family, friends and co-workers. Information networks encompass the spread of information, rumours or even diseases. Biological networks often look at proteins, genes and the way they interact and there are many other types of network. Researchers can look at centrality measures, to identify the important nodes in a network; clustering, which is finding groups of closely connected nodes; path analysis to determine the shortest path between nodes; and community detection, or identifying subgroups within a network.

The posts, tweets and other annotations made visible via user-generated content allows patterns and correlations to be revealed that might, in other circumstances, remain unnoticed (Chan, Zeng and Schäfer, 2022). Twitter and Facebook in particular offered almost real-time insights into emerging health conditions, clusters and attitudes towards public health messages and vaccination, as was very apparent during the COVID-19 pandemic first identified in 2019.

Whatever method is used, it is vital that ethical guidelines and principles are adhered to, all necessary permissions are confirmed and, above all, user privacy is respected.

Social media and the dissemination of healthcare research results

When it comes to disseminating the results of research, there are several options, including those that incorporate social media features. Social media can offer a cost-effective method of disseminating research results once a study is complete or has reached its time limit. Some of these involve specific academic social media platforms such as ResearchGate, Semantic Scholar, Mendeley, Zotero and Academia.edu, also sometimes referred to as academic social networks (ASNs). Jordan (2019) has identified the evolution of this type of social media site, as they increasingly represent an alternative and even competition to traditional publishing options. Some of these, notably Mendeley and Zotero, double as reference management software. The uses of these types of social media platforms can include identifying potential research partners as well as building a picture of the work of a particular researcher.

Since social media first became a phenomenon, new platforms and adaptations have surfaced with regularity. While many are text-based, some others incorporate visual elements, notably Connected Papers (Behera, Jain and Kumar, 2023).

Bibliometrics and altmetrics

These ASNs also offer a citation analysis alternative to some of the traditional tools like Web of Science and Scopus. Researchers may track the number of their citations as well as, in some cases, respond to comments and direct messages from fellow researchers. It is often also possible to use 'social tagging' to add user-driven keywords, build a personalised library and store academic papers in a relatively systematic way.

Rather than likes and shares, metrics on ASNs often incorporate more academic metrics. On ResearchGate, for example, these include citations, recommendations, reads and their proprietary 'Research Interest Score'. Academia.edu incorporates details of papers written by individual researchers, numbers of followers and views. Mendeley incorporates information on citations and readers. Once a citation is saved to an individual's library, real-language tags can be added, in a variation on social bookmarking. While general social bookmarking may not be as popular as it was in the early days of social media, social citations and tagging remain a highly useful tool in healthcare research. This is despite the demise of some earlier apps such as Connotea and CiteULike and the acquisition of Colwiz by the Taylor & Francis publishing group (Wood, 2017).

In a world where the ability to demonstrate impact, and help users demonstrate their academic or scientific impact, is increasingly important to ensure the survival of an information service, the use of metrics from ASNs can be a cost-effective option to use instead of, or as well as, similar features from Web of Science and Scopus.

Assessing the impact of healthcare research often requires a more sophisticated approach than simple numbers of citations, although bibliometrics can be a useful if blunt tool to measure impact. Sometimes called citation metrics, bibliometrics measure references between published works or citations, the theory being that these citations indicate a particular level of both influence and interest amongst scholars. The 'standard' bibliometrics tools usually incorporate data from one of the large databases of citations: Web of Science; Scopus; or Google Scholar.

On academic social networks, an alternative type of bibliometric known as altmetrics is often used. This approach is increasingly seen in online journal articles such as those published by the BMJ. Altmetrics data is a 'simple and effective way of understanding who is engaging with research online' as well as what they're saying (Altmetric, 2024). The take-up of altmetrics, however, has been somewhat slow compared to more traditional bibliometrics.

Measuring the impact of altmetrics

Measuring the impact of research on social media, whether it is in terms of how successful the recruitment has been, or how widely the results have been disseminated and shared, can be difficult. While altmetrics, described as a 'system that tracks the attention that research outputs such as scholarly articles and data sets receive online' can help to measure reach, establishing the actual impact of research is a little more complex. Pulido et al. (2018), for example, have concentrated on the social impact of research, while Chavda and Patel (2016) point out that altmetrics alone are not enough to measure the academic impact of research.

Social media platforms such as blogs, Twitter (X), Facebook and article reference managers such as Mendeley are also now being used to communicate and discuss research. Altmetrics, short for 'alternative metrics' was first described by Priem, Groth and Taraborelli (2012) and is a term used for 'web-based metrics'. This example of how social media has changed and modernised the way in which academic impact is measured is, however, not without controversy. What has been highlighted, however, is that it is no longer enough to rely only on impact factors which can be regarded as a somewhat outdated method: this is 'the ratio of citations received to articles published by a journal and purports to represent the prestige and value of a scholarly journal' (Nestor et al., 2020).

Some studies have found moderate correlations between some altmetrics and traditional citation counts, suggesting they capture distinct aspects of research impact (Priem, Groth and Taraborelli, 2012). As we have already seen, different social media platforms attract varying demographics of researchers and serve different purposes in scholarly communication (Mehrazar et al., 2018). While altmetrics show some promise in providing a more comprehensive view of research impact, questions remain about their underlying meaning and validity (Holmberg, 2014). As the scholarly community increasingly integrates social media into professional communications, altmetrics offer potential for broader and faster measures of impact, complementing rather than replacing traditional citation metrics in research evaluation (Priem, Groth and Taraborelli, 2012; Chavda and Patel, 2016).

Overall, social media has demonstrated its potential value in healthcare research, complementing more traditional methods of information dissemination as well as research subject engagement. Social media has emerged as a particularly promising tool for recruiting research participants, offering cost-effective and efficient access to diverse populations, including hard-to-reach groups (Jones, Wilson-Keates and Melrose, 2024). While some studies have found social media to be the most effective recruitment method, particularly for observational studies and hard-to-reach populations, results are mixed regarding its overall effectiveness compared to traditional methods (Topolovec-Vranic and Natarajan, 2016).

Generating ideas for healthcare research on social media

Analysis of social media data can also highlight gaps in research, while official accounts for organisations such as the National Institute for Health and Care Research (usually shortened to NIHR), the UK government funding body, and other funding bodies can also ensure that their calls for research bids reach the widest population possible. There is another aspect of social media in research that has not had as much attention in the literature as some others, namely the potential of posts and tweets to help to identify gaps in the literature and act as a catalyst for research ideas. D'Souza, Hooten and Murad (2021) have highlighted how important it is to frame research questions, identify the most appropriate social media outlet and select content.

Some authors, such as Mahdavi Ardestani et al. (2023) have attempted to address the research gap, particularly in the wake of COVID-19. During the COVID-19 pandemic, barriers to the provision and use of online learning in medical and healthcare settings were highlighted, including the digital divide. Some students were easily able to access high-end technology while others were not.

Monitoring health and research trends on social media

Clinical professionals and healthcare information professionals alike can, however, use social media to share educational ideas, opportunities for networking and insights into data via social media. In healthcare settings, the insights into patient care that can be provided are invaluable.

According to Awurdi (2019) healthcare surveillance means that professionals are able to monitor trends in disease on social media, while Danbaki et al. (2020) have identified the ease with which stakeholders are able to stay informed about news, research and trends in healthcare. Librarians can help users ensure that any information that is shared is evidence-based and, where it diverges from current consensus, any underlying reasons are robust and methodologically sound (Jeyaraman et al., 2023).

Issues and controversies around using social media for healthcare research

In addition to the practicalities of whether participants and potential participants are able to access social media in the first place, there are further issues to consider.

Some of these centre on the uploading or publication of content which could potentially breach patient confidentiality or copyright, as well as the potential for reputational damage if negative comments are posted. As mentioned earlier, researchers must also be on the lookout for fake participants: on social media and the internet in general, anyone can literally be anything they choose. Sponsorship of potential research candidates by companies or other vested interests is another potential controversy that researchers may need to take into account (Wellman et al., 2020).

The dissemination of research results via social media is another area that can be unexpectedly contentious. We could reasonably hope that research, once complete and in the public domain, would be robust until the circumstance of subsequent evidence should come to light. The numbers of retracted papers, however, indicate otherwise. In 2023 alone, over 10,000 papers were retracted (Van Noorden, 2023). Social media can also offer a responsive and cost-effective channel to disseminate this information.

Retraction of research

Healthcare research is an extremely dynamic specialism and as new evidence comes to light, research is often contradicted, clarified, overturned or even retracted. Retraction Watch, itself a social media organisation, being both a blog and a database, is used by some of the social sharing sites mentioned earlier, notably Zotero, to flag retracted papers such as this (Brainard, 2023).

During the pandemic, the importance of preprint servers also came to the forefront. There was also concern about the use of bots or AI in the production of posts, predatory journals and the proliferation of preprints that had not gone through any peer review process.

Social media often comes in for criticism as a purveyor of misinformation. It can, however, also act as an early warning of research papers that, at best, lack cohesion or, at worst, are misleading or can even be potentially dangerous.

The Surgisphere scandal, which will be covered in more detail in Chapter 6, is one particularly high-profile example (Servick and Enserink, 2020). The probable spurious nature of the data and the recommendations was identified by writers on social media. The investigation uncovered inconsistencies so stark that papers in *The New England Journal of Medicine* and *The Lancet* had to be retracted.

Social media in healthcare research: roles for healthcare information professionals

One of the most challenging aspects of researching can be how to stay ahead of the way in which fields of study are developing. Healthcare information professionals are well placed to assist with many aspects of using social media to support healthcare research. This may involve horizon scanning and traditional searching using social media to identify funding opportunities, identifying areas where there are gaps and/or oversaturation and ensuring accurate records of searches are maintained. These records may include subsequent citations of the work of researchers and, crucially, any measurable or clearly demonstrated impact on patient care, policy or public health messaging.

While 'credibility of information' has been cited as a major concern around the way that tools like Google and Wikipedia are used by junior clinicians, Hughes et al. (2009) noted that these types of tools were used at least three times as frequently as the National Library of Medicine's PubMed site. Health sciences librarians are well placed to offer education and guidance in how to assess the credibility of social media, in the same way that critical appraisal often now features in the instruction programmes of many libraries.

Healthcare information professionals may also be able to assist with data cleaning. One option is for a member of the research team – possibly the supporting librarian – to join the research study directly and manually collect data. There are, as always, ethical considerations to bear in mind, particularly where patient data or contact features. In addition, this approach can be very labour-intensive, including deduplication and tidying.

Librarians can, therefore, maximise their input by also helping to advise on the most appropriate data analysis techniques. This may include content analysis, sentiment analysis or network analysis, amongst others.

Roles for librarians in this area, besides the traditional literature searching input, may also include helping users to select the most appropriate social media platform to use for recruitment. Other considerations include ensuring that any legal and ethical frameworks are in place, so that privacy and confidentiality are maintained. Finally, healthcare information professionals are well placed to assist not only with the analysis but the dissemination of the research once completed.

CHAPTER 5

The Use of Social Media in Medical Education

Introduction

Although a small number of healthcare libraries had already experimented with using a social media platform or delivery method for educational opportunities and information, it was during COVID-19 in particular that social media came into its own in this respect. Social media lends itself well to synchronous remote learning as well as video sessions, flipped classrooms, virtual classrooms and e-learning (Fouasson-Chailloux et al., 2022).

Healthcare information professionals may often find themselves able to use social media to contribute in the realm of medical education, from delivery to analysis of feedback. In addition to suggesting appropriate social media tools for a given task, there are also specific areas where social media can support the creation of educational resources and where healthcare librarians can assist. Benchmarking searches to uncover innovative uses of social media in other organisations are another potentially beneficial way in which librarians can contribute.

Social media in its current form is not, however, suitable as an acquisition method for all skills. Gheshlagh et al. (2022) were amongst those who highlighted the current inadequacy of online methods as an option to acquire practical skills. Other factors highlighted in this study included lack of responses or answers from educators. A further finding which is particularly interesting in a healthcare context where interpersonal relationships are the lifeblood of many interactions is that the use of social media occasioned, for some, a perception of 'coldness' in the educator/trainee relationship.

When it comes to e-learning in particular, although Web 2.0 technologies have shown great promise since the early years (Blaum et al., 2013), a decade later the barriers to accessing these relatively advanced technologies remain significant in some healthcare settings and will be considered in more detail in Chapter 7 on barriers (Mahdavi et al., 2023).

Library support for healthcare education via social media

Henner (2023) identified that librarians, too, may be feeling a sense of disconnect in the wake of COVID-19. In the early years of social media, Connell (2009) carried out research into the opinions of students with regards to librarians on Facebook. At the time, Twitter was the channel used least extensively by medical school librarians in the UK. Where libraries were using this channel, it was often to announce opening hours, updates with electronic services and news items. Feedback from students about Twitter was mixed, with some expressing ambivalence about how useful a tool it was for their course, despite sometimes using Twitter or another tool for social networking (Minocha, 2009).

In 2009, the majority of communication on medical education courses still occurred in face-to-face settings. It is not only in medical education where social media is a potentially useful tool; it has also made its presence felt in nursing education. Vanzetta et al. (2016) are, however, amongst those who have highlighted the importance of both ensuring the privacy of personal data and the safety of the learning environment.

Social media platforms to support writing for education and publication: wikis and blogs

Writing papers for publication is an area which can often straddle both research and education. Since assistance with writing for education and/or publication is another area where librarians can often offer constructive input, the most appropriate tools for this would often fall under the heading of either blogging or wikis. These may be openly available, in the public domain, or controlled by passwords and logins. Blogger, Tumblr and WordPress are examples of blogging tools that are often found in educational settings. Users may subscribe to RSS feeds so they can stay up-to-date with new posts and updates on information, while librarians can help advise on the compilation, tagging and overall management of blog posts.

Wikis, of which the most famous is Wikipedia, are similar to blogging sites. Although this is a generalisation, they are not updated with new posts or articles quite as frequently, although existing content may be frequently revised and amended. Wikis are also usually linked by specific disciplines or subject areas. They can be used as a relatively passive source of information or a more active tool for students to assess, correct and update content, as described by Maggio et al. (2020). In health sciences, wikis have been used for data collection, group projects, repositories of institutional publications and grey literature, collections of procedures, interventions and case studies.

Blog posts and wiki entries may also be used as teaching aids, subject to the same critical appraisal considerations as any other social media site or post. Librarians may find it beneficial to their users to run a blog with updates on new services and acquisitions, literature searching tips, or links to new guidelines. It's often possible to incorporate multimedia content, whether images, sound files, presentations from sites such as SlideShare, or video content from Vimeo or YouTube, used with appropriate permissions.

A blog may also be used as file repositories for short-term projects or meetings details. The commenting features, if not turned off, can help to support community engagement and in addition widgets can be embedded, with the purpose of, for example, drawing in RSS feeds. The addition of widgets can turn blogs into information hubs. Another feature of some social media sites is the option to auto-post content to other channels, helping to minimise the amount of staff time required for administration.

Blogs can also support the delivery of medical education that is free and open access or even the creation of learning portfolios. One of the strengths of social media is also, paradoxically, one of its main weaknesses. There are no quality controls on the opinions or information posted, although some sentiments may be followed up if they fall into the category of hate crimes or other responses that are deemed inappropriate.

In some cases, blogs have been used as part of a course assignment (Schlegel and Primacio, 2021) and to save case studies (suitably anonymised) as a future study resource (Thaung, 2018). Patient blogs can also be an unexpected source of insight into and education about how particular conditions affect individuals (Taylor and Humphrey, 2021).

Learner engagement and feedback on social media

While quantitative measures of engagement with social media are relatively easy to assess (Sigerson and Cheng, 2018), via for example likes, reposts and shares and even comments, there are relatively few objective methods of obtaining comparative feedback. There is currently relatively little overarching cohesive research into the effects and impact of incorporating social media into classroom education, although some librarians have had success with developing courses to support specific course needs at their organisation (Cobus-Kuo, 2011).

Another aspect of using social media in healthcare education that is slightly undersung is the relative ease with which feedback can be collected, collated and analysed. This can assist healthcare professionals and librarians alike in facilitating training needs analysis research. In addition, this can provide evidence for the design of subsequent user education programmes.

Many social media platforms are designed to engage learners, just as they engage users in general, although each platform has its own specific strengths. YouTube, for example, is often used for teaching technical skills, with the facility to add subtitles, repeat sequences and home in on particular features. Dentists in particular have acknowledged its usefulness (Fu et al., 2022), although sometimes with caveats (Dias da Silva, Pereira and Walmsley, 2019). In some parts of the world, for example Saudi Arabia, YouTube is the most commonly used social media platform in medical education (Khanagar et al., 2022). Blogs and wikis have also been used to beneficial effect in higher education in the medical field, helping to encourage active collaboration and knowledge sharing as well as professional reflection, which is an essential part of professional development.

Some universities also regularly make use of social media to create virtual classrooms and increase access to academic libraries. Older-style massive open online courses (MOOCs) may have given way to platforms such as Blackboard and discovery systems, but the principles remain the same. The key is to engage the learner. This engagement may be with the content, with peers, with the educator, or all three.

Evaluating the impact of social media in healthcare education

What remains difficult to evaluate is the effectiveness of using social media in health education. This is compounded by the fact that in many studies clear comparative groups are lacking. What is not in doubt is that social media is one of the innovations that has dramatically transformed the way in which people connect with each other, participate in learning and network (De Gagne et al., 2018). Up until the pandemic, the use of social media in education was still developing and hindered by the lack of clear policies around its use (Price et al., 2018).

Prensky (2001) also highlighted the fact that traditional education systems are no longer suitable for today's students, who increasingly expect to be able to study remotely, at a time convenient to them. Indeed, during the pandemic lockdowns of 2020 to 2022, there was often little or no choice. In many cases, students were only able to learn online.

This is a great contrast to previous opinions on the topic. Despite the benefits of SoMe as Elliott (2014) referred to it, when it comes to professional development and the training of educators, the research in the mid-2010s also found that some researchers claimed social media in education was unnecessary. Not only that, it was potentially a distraction for students who were already overworked.

The demographics of the users of social media should be borne in mind when deciding what platform to use; over 80% of students in healthcare belong to Generation Z or, at their older end of their age range, millennials, who have never known a life without the internet (Duke et al., 2017). For Stephens and Gunther (2016), millennials have very distinctive styles of learning from digital immigrants.

Although there is immense potential in the use of social media as an educational tool, to some extent they remain an underutilised educational resource for students, trainees, doctors in training and residents and for the consultants and trainers teaching them. In a world where cost is often a consideration, social media offers a cost-effective, if not free, method of accessing educational opportunities. This includes peer-to-peer learning.

Social media and the effect on hierarchies in learning

One aspect of social media that is also little discussed is its effect on hierarchies, official or otherwise, in learning experience. In a physical classroom, more extroverted students will often tend to dominate whereas in online settings, more introverted students may flourish (de Jongh and de la Croix, 2016).

WhatsApp, for example, was highlighted in a 2015 study as 'flattening' the hierarchy among students, residents and experienced consultants. For those who are shy or neurodiverse, an online environment may be effective in allowing them to contribute to discussions in a more uninhibited manner, allowing them time to formulate their response, rather than having to respond to the 'traditional' approach of putting learners on the spot or 'pimping' (Duong, 2021).

Mobile learning in healthcare and medical education

A further benefit of social media, combined with modern smartphones, means that, as long as learners can get a reliable signal, learning is no longer limited to the classroom, ward or lab; it can take place anywhere (Farsi, 2021).

The majority of medical schools in the UK are attached to a major university or other educational establishment and academic institutions have generally been at the forefront of technological advancements (Humphreys, 2019). Long before the COVID-19 pandemic, it was apparent that the social characteristics of Web 2.0 made it particularly appropriate where students needed to fit studies around the unsociable hours that are often a feature of studying medicine. Where students are on placement a long distance away from their seat of study, social media and Web 2.0 can offer something of a remedy, if only partial, to the geographical isolation of such placements. The shift in the role of clinical educators was identified as far back as 2009 (Minocha, 2009) and information literacy had already been noted as a concern, following Kamel Boulos and Wheeler's understanding of the potential for Web 2.0 as a tool in clinician education and training (2007).

Social media and health literacy

For healthcare information professionals, this is an area where it is possible to offer expertise and input, acting as champions and helping to bridge the gap between the complex medical information and jargon often used by healthcare professionals and simpler ways of expressing those ideas to aid patient understanding. In some organisations, librarians have direct responsibility for helping patients to find and understand information and in these cases, professional skills can be put to good use to navigate health information online as well as distinguish the credible sources from the less credible.

Knowledge transfer is another area that can benefit from the input of a healthcare information professional, as evidence-based research is shared with healthcare providers with the aim of informing patient care.

Other authors, including Vukušić Rukavina et al. (2021) have also highlighted issues around the potential of unprofessional behaviour. Incivility on social media has been highlighted (Guy et al., 2023), with the solution felt to be adopting strategies to encourage civility. Some nursing schools have even introduced cyber civility guidelines (De Gagne et al., 2018). Librarians can help by signposting users to methods of combating this behaviour implemented successfully in other organisations. In the early days of the internet, there was a great deal of discussion around the appropriate way to behave online, or 'netiquette', as it was sometimes called.

Using images from social media in healthcare education

In many cases, healthcare professionals require images or multimedia to support their teaching. Finding appropriate images to support instruction is just one area where social media can be of great use.

Finding images that are not subject to copyright is often difficult, however. One way around this is to use photo-sharing sites, including Flickr, Unsplash and Pixabay as well as Wikimedia Commons. Some images can be reused under Creative Commons licences. All of these are areas where healthcare librarians can assist, both in finding the images or clips in the first place and in ensuring that healthcare professionals are complying with copyright.

This can be a little more difficult with content that is user-generated by those who may not be experts or may not understand the implications of sharing their content (or indeed, that of others). While TikTok is the current platform of choice for short videos, for example, librarians may need to guide students and healthcare professionals to ensure that they are using images that are ethically generated, accurate and do not infringe copyright or other legislation. It is all too easy to 'borrow' an image or a meme without giving due accreditation.

Social media in patient education

Social media can also be used as a method of patient education (Wojtara, 2023), although relatively few formal patient education or information officer posts appear to be specifically occupied by librarians. For Kauffman, Weisberg and Fishman (2022), as has been highlighted already, TikTok is the most rapidly growing social media app in the world. Despite the fact they were only able to identify a relatively small number of professional education videos, it was clear that the platform was more than just a 'silly dancing app'. Kirkpatrick and Lawrie (2024) agree on the speed with which TikTok is gaining social media market share and have identified the importance of the platform for healthcare information, for young women in particular. The body of research evidence around the effectiveness of the platform and methods for the acquisition of clinical skills, however, remains somewhat scant and has been identified as a research gap (Tsapatsoulis and Djouvas, 2019).

There was also an awareness of the fact that social media offered the chance for educators to reach substantial audiences, especially in the early years of education, as long as it was used with a degree of caution (Kauffman, Weisberg and Fishman, 2022).

Social media as a tool for microlearning

While, at present, the pedagogical landscape does not easily allow for full-length educational experiences on social media, at least where practical skills are taught and assessed, social media can be extremely rewarding for what Conde-Caballero et al. (2023) refer to as 'microlearning' in education.

Conde-Caballero et al. (2023) used a particular approach known as the Technology Acceptance Model (TAM) to evaluate the perceptions of students undertaking a bachelor's degree in nursing. They discovered high levels of satisfaction and engagement, with the results not showing variations relating specifically to gender differences, but slight variations depending on the subject. This may be at least in part due to the demographics of those on the course and whether they are what Prensky (2001) calls 'digital natives' or 'digital immigrants'. To recap, 'digital natives' are usually deemed to be those born after 1980, who have never really known a world without the internet. This particularly applies to Generation Z. What are termed 'digital immigrants', on the other hand, are those who had to adapt to technology later in life. In generational terms, this term encompasses Boomers; Generation X; and earlier Millennials. Where older generations have had to adapt and actively incorporate social media into their workflows, this has often been due to the careers chosen. Healthcare librarianship, for instance, involves the need for a high level of technical skills in many cases, resulting in the 'early adoption' of technologies mentioned earlier.

Medical schools and Web 2.0 for engagement with library users

In the early years of Web 2.0, several university medical schools were amongst those who were swift to adopt these new approaches and technologies. Swansea School of Health Science, for example, established a blog hosted on the blogging service WordPress. All posts were tagged to allow readers to link to posts from other blogs covering the same topic and Really Simple Syndication (RSS) feeds were incorporated from relevant sites. Posts covered practical user information, including opening hours, interlibrary loans, study skills, information on relevant resources and health news stories as well as links to clips from radio and video. At the time of writing, the blog no longer exists, having been deleted – something of an occupational hazard of the internet. In a world where it is extremely easy to post content, it is equally easy to delete it.

Hull York Medical School Blog, another of the new medical schools set up in 2003, also posted a blog, this time hosted by 'Blogger', an alternative to WordPress, with archives going back to August 2008. In this case, posts were not tagged or categorised. The content was not dissimilar to that produced by Swansea and included details of opening hours, database trials, access to e-journals, library surveys and other general topics. The page was run as a 'news' page rather than as a place where two-way communication with students could occur. The blog remains available at http://hymslibrary.blogspot.com.

The University of Sheffield blog at www.librarydevelopmentgroup.shef.ac.uk/blogs/meddent was maintained by the Faculty Librarian, using a version of WordPress that had been installed on a university server. It was customised and adapted to represent the library at the university. There were additional pages describing the blog, its contributors and archives as far back as January 2008. Keywords were used to tag all posts, with links to external sites and the Twitter stream for the university. This blog also had relatively little two-way communication with students, although when a competition was run giving anyone who commented the opportunity to win an iPod, engagement increased. Minocha (2009) also noted that other comments on the blog were used to influence the provision of the library's services. This site was also unreachable at the time of writing.

Using social media in education: overcoming the pitfalls

Despite the potential pitfalls of using social media in healthcare education, there are many authors that hold the position that the advantages outweigh the disadvantages (Bernhardt, Alber and Gold, 2014).

One solution is for healthcare professionals to use online professional communities as a kind of 'halfway house/safe space' between social networking and professional networking. This type of platform often has higher levels of security attached than 'open' social media (Murad et al., 2019). Marshal et al. (2021) are amongst those who have outlined the need for a separation online between content that is personal and content that is professional.

For Mouelhi et al. (2017), there is a need for accessible information which is easy to find – another area where healthcare librarians can put their traditional classification skills or their more recently acquired metadata skills to good use. Healthcare librarians can 'leverage' social media in education through various strategies, including the establishment of clear policies and guidelines (Elliott, 2014). In addition to supporting evidence-based clinical practice, social media offers the opportunity to increase the engagement of stakeholders (Price et al., 2018).

CHAPTER 6

COVID-19 and Misinformation on Social Media

Misinformation before COVID-19

While COVID-19 is the most recent and startling example of misinformation having been spread by social media, it's far from the first. In fact, between 2006 and 2017, false news stories travelled faster than true news stories on Twitter (Vosoughi, Roy and Aral, 2018). While the majority of misinformation relating to COVID-19 was found on Facebook, Twitter and TikTok, another type of social media was far from immune: virtual worlds. Second Life, a virtual world launched in 2003 by Linden Lab, initially gained popularity as a platform for businesses and social interaction (Müller and Koschate, 2012). Despite its early promise, Second Life's success has been limited due to low active user numbers and challenges in finding trustworthy information (Suomi, Mäntymäki and Söderlund, 2014).

Mumps, measles and rubella

The belief in the combined MMR (mumps, measles and rubella) vaccination is another severe case of misinformation. Despite the fact that Andrew Wakefield, the doctor who put forward the original theory in 1998 has long since been discredited and struck off the UK medical register, the harm was already done. Vaccine scepticism increased in the wake of the publication (Motta and Stecula, 2021) and despite the retraction, Wakefield continues to be quoted by the anti-vaccine lobby.

For Gabarron, Oyeyemi and Wynn (2021), while misinformation might be a particular concern for the general public, healthcare providers themselves can also, on occasion, be responsible for spreading misinformation. Healthcare librarians have a responsibility in this area: namely, dispelling the misinformation or disinformation that was so prevalent during the COVID-19 pandemic and ensuring that accurate resources are made accessible instead. In addition, our responsibilities extend to ensuring that users have appropriate levels of health literacy, or specifically health information literacy.

The COVID-19 pandemic

When historians come to write the annals of the first quarter of the 21st century, one of the defining events will be the COVID-19 pandemic and its effect on every aspect of our lives: social, educational, health, economic and societal. We are still in the early stages of understanding how the pandemic has changed our society.

For the 30 years prior to the pandemic, people had been increasingly using the internet to find information about their health, as was evident in Google Trends data and other sources of information. COVID-19 was officially identified by the World Health Organization in winter 2019 following an outbreak of 'pneumonia of unknown origin' (Dwyer, 2023). It was declared a pandemic in January 2020. For almost two years, much of the world effectively closed down, forcing many of us to find new ways of learning, socialising and conducting our daily business, from grocery shopping to work to leisure.

Social media at its simplest can be a great information equaliser. Text can be communicated even in low-resource settings. One of the strengths of social media is, however, also its fatal flaw, sometimes literally: anyone can create and share content. According to Allcott, Gentzkow and Yu (2019), one of the most concerning aspects of social media is its potential for use in spreading fake news, along with the possibility of negative effects on society in general, the decisions people make and the behaviours they display.

During the pandemic, particularly in the early stages, social media often became one of the few information sources available – for good and ill. It was often used to disseminate public health messages and in an attempt to lift morale. Stories that 'went viral' included the case of Captain Tom walking laps of his Bedfordshire garden to raise funds for the NHS; the 45th President of the United States endorsing hydroxychloroquine as a cure for COVID; and the intriguing case of Surgisphere, a tiny US-based company which claimed to have access to huge amounts of data on the emerging novel coronavirus (Davey, Kirchgaessner and Boseley, 2020).

Misinformation in COVID-19

The COVID-19 pandemic was frequently compared to the Great Influenza Epidemic of 1918–20 (Liang, Liang and Rosen, 2021; van Doren, 2021; He et al., 2020). The way that information was disseminated during that epidemic, however, was mostly through the mainstream media.

During COVID-19, social media was something of a double-edged sword. On the one hand, it was a way for Public Health England (now the United Kingdom Health Security Agency, UKHSA) and other organisations to get information out to millions of people quickly and accurately. It also offered a way to track the uptake of vaccinations (Garett and Young, 2022), to spread both correct and incorrect information about vaccine side effects (Lentzen et al., 2022) and to use sentiment analysis techniques to track responses to the vaccination programme (Iwendi et al., 2022).

As technology continues to advance and become ever more complex, guidelines around its use require ongoing modification. Healthcare professionals also have a responsibility to use social media in a responsible manner to maintain the trust of the public. As well as patient or service user privacy and confidentiality and copyright law, there are disclosure rules to obey: local, regional, national or international. During COVID-19, some of the usual rules appeared to become somewhat fluid.

Social media also offered an opportunity for healthcare professionals to tell their side of the story (Pangborn et al., 2021). This was despite the fact, as subsequent television dramas such as *Breathtaking* have shown, there were often attempts by senior management to close down any dissent. Social media therefore offered a way for clinicians to express their concern about many aspects of how the pandemic was being managed.

Many governments were as honest as they could be with their populations, with some countries such as New Zealand (Beattie and Priestley, 2021) being exceptionally truthful and most countries achieving at least a reasonable level of trust (Lim et al., 2021), there were some surprising exceptions. Trust in government messages in England, for example, sank to particular lows following the first wave (Boehm et al., 2023). Gabarron, Oyeyemi and Wynn (2021) discovered that misinformation around the condition was rife on social media. Depending on the platform, these posts ranged from 0.2% to 28.8% of posts, with just some of the topics including statistics around the disease, treatments, methods of prevention and information about how the disease was transmitted. In addition to its role as a rapid method of disseminating official information about public health, social media was also only too efficient a method to spread misinformation. The spread of misinformation across social media resulted in fear and panic. Some suggested strategies to combat this proliferation of misinformation included ensuring that messages were evidence-based and an active presence of health professionals on social platforms. Improving the health literacy levels of the public was another possible technique.

Thousands of papers were published on the 'novel coronavirus' as scientists and medics attempted to understand the outbreak. Between 2019 and the time of writing in July 2024, over 21,275 papers on PubMed alone are tagged with either COVID-19 misinformation or COVID-19 'fake news'. Over 31,100 of those were published in 2021 or 2022. While clinical professionals are, in many cases, extremely aware of the need for critical appraisal, health literacy amongst the general public has been highlighted as an issue many times (Whitney, Keselman and Humphreys, 2017).

Can we trust social media?

While 'expert by experience' is a relatively recent term, social media users need to know how trustworthy the content they're consuming, and often sharing, really is. One of the areas where social media can potentially be used for the power of good is where healthcare information professionals are involved in disseminating the message, potentially resulting in raised levels of healthcare literacy amongst the general public. This assumes, of course, that the healthcare professional involved is themselves trustworthy: social media users need to apply critical thinking skills to understand whether what they are reading is credible and accurate.

In the case of the COVID-19 pandemic in particular, social messaging service X (Twitter) provided an instant stream of information flowing between people around the world. Its short, often pithy posts were easy to digest, even on the simplest of devices. Users were able to follow health conferences, a developing health story, search for information or share web links instantly from their desks or mobile devices. Searching for any topic on Twitter, health-related or otherwise, leads to new contacts, networks and information.

Alongside Twitter (X), there are countless blogs on health topics written by specialists and non-specialists alike that are read, commented on and shared globally. How credible and accurate are they? If they are objectively so and the data can be corroborated with information from trustworthy sources, they should be encouraged and supported.

Social networks such as Facebook or American social networking site Hi5 have been used by hundreds of millions of people to communicate about a huge range of topics, including health. Type 'malaria' or 'maternal mortality' into a search engine and Wikipedia, the online encyclopaedia that anyone can edit, is likely to be the first entry referenced.

Social media also allows visuals of unusual health events to be published minutes or even seconds after they've taken place. The integrated and often surprisingly powerful cameras now integrated into many mobile phones also dramatically increase the numbers of potential publishers around the world. YouTube or Flickr, video and photo sites have millions of users and where particular clips or information are shared rapidly, it's said to have 'gone viral'.

Critical appraisal of social media

While critical appraisal has always been a feature of higher medical education and, increasingly, other disciplines like nursing and physiotherapy, when analysing social media content, clinical professionals need to exercise even higher levels of discrimination. One of the strengths of social media also contains the seeds of its downfall, namely that in most cases the content has not been reviewed, let alone peer reviewed. The influence of potential bias is one factor to consider, along with, in some cases, cultural or linguistic considerations. At the height of COVID-19, this need for judicious analysis was highlighted in the ways that world governments handled their information campaigns around the virus, the development of the vaccine and the vaccination rollout and the social, economic and educational fallout.

Some of the other misinformation that surfaced on social media during the pandemic included the effectiveness or otherwise of mask wearing, the efficacy of vaccinations and even xenophobia against certain groups or nationalities.

There were, however, some differences in the ways in which information about COVID-19 spread on the various social networks.

Information about COVID-19 on various social networks

Facebook

As might be expected from the largest social media platform in the world, Facebook played a significant role in disseminating information about COVID-19, serving as a platform for health agencies, individuals and various organisations to share content (Kiran, 2022; Ahmed et al., 2020). While it facilitated communication and support networks during the pandemic (Fernandes et al., 2020), the platform was also, in some cases, a source of misinformation. Studies have found that a considerable portion of COVID-19-related posts on two of the most popular platforms, Facebook and Twitter (X), contained unverifiable or false information (Ahmed et al., 2020). The pandemic had been incorporated into diverse agendas, including political attacks, donation solicitations and business promotions (Mejova and Kalimeri, 2020).

In some cases, Facebook advertisements were used to spread conspiracy theories and unverified claims about the virus (Mejova and Kalimeri, 2020). Despite these challenges, Facebook also offered a space for sharing personal experiences, seeking support and raising awareness about COVID-19 (Kiran, 2022), highlighting the complex role of social media during public health crises.

Instagram

Compared to analysis of COVID-19 misinformation on Facebook and Twitter, Instagram has received relatively little attention in the published literature, and where there are exceptions, Instagram has formed part of the consideration (Adebesin, 2023). There are other studies, however, where the general accuracy of information on Instagram comes under scrutiny. When Ramasubramanian et al. (2023) analysed the accuracy of posts on Instagram on stroke, for instance, over 88% of the posts were factually accurate. This was despite the fact that contributions from healthcare professionals were far from extensive. Although Instagram is an important platform for healthcare information, others are more popular. While the popularity of social media is very apparent in the population at large, it has taken a little longer to find its place in healthcare information. When von Muhlen and Ohno-Machado conducted their systematic review (2012), they also discovered that social media use amongst students and healthcare professionals was increasing, with Facebook continuing to dominate as the most frequently used social media platform.

TikTok

While Facebook, Instagram, Twitter and YouTube retained their influence, it was during the pandemic that TikTok in particular also came under scrutiny for spreading misinformation.

During the pandemic, social media also provided an outlet for the experiences of healthcare workers, with Al-Rawi and Zemenchik (2023) identifying four distinct topics. These included the mental health and working conditions of healthcare workers; appreciation of healthcare 'heroes'; criticism of official authorities and their messaging; countering and contradicting misinformation; approaching an extraordinarily serious situation with humour or satire; and content with an educational message.

Ostrovsky and Chen (2020) found out that only 6.44% of videos were filmed by healthcare professionals, although they were often 'liked' the most frequently and shared across the board. As well as a channel for spreading information about COVID-19, TikTok also offered the chance for practitioners to redress any misconceptions about the condition, even potentially reaching those who might not be easy to reach otherwise. Ostrovsky and Chen are also amongst those who have identified TikTok as a potentially important platform for healthcare professionals and institutions to promote correct information about conditions.

The importance of hashtags as a signpost to social content during COVID-19 was particularly apparent on Instagram, Twitter and TikTok, where the hashtag #WearAMask attracted over 500 million views during COVID. WHO-posted videos attracted almost 57 million hits. One of the salient differences was the use of humour; 68% of the trending videos with the #WearAMask hashtag incorporated humour, while only 9% of the videos originating from the WHO contained humour (Basch et al., 2021).

For some, however, displays of humour on the part of healthcare professionals on social media during the pandemic were regarded as inappropriate, particularly where the personal and public persona of the healthcare professionals in question appeared to be at odds.

During the pandemic, a time of both higher than usual stress and lower than usual levels of social interaction, some clinicians turned to social media platforms as a way to express and process their emotions. TikTok was one of the particular platforms of choice, although the mainstream media often chose to focus on some of the more controversial clips, with newspapers like the *Daily Mail* highlighting the frivolous nature of nurses dancing in uniform. There's a lesson for healthcare information professionals, however, in helping their users to understand how TikTok can be used to communicate with the public on health issues of importance (Yalamanchili et al., 2022).

Weibo

In some countries, the restrictions on the use of social media were notable from an early stage. Towards the beginning of the outbreak, Dr Li Wenliang, a Wuhan-based Chinese doctor, used his Weibo social media channel as a way to try to warn the public about COVID-19. The Chinese government at the time was attempting to minimise the virus, designating it as just another 'common flu' virus. The doctor disappeared from his social media soon after he had attempted to warn the world. Tragically, he eventually died from the virus.

Even in the UK and other countries, some commentators raised concerns around clinicians who took to social media to raise the alarm about issues such as PPE shortages (Hoernke et al., 2021; Law, Kanagasingam and Choong, 2021). There was concern in some cases about whether some of these clinicians would have faced investigations around 'fitness to practise' standards in the UK (Richard et al., 2014). Some clinicians even found themselves the targets of attacks (Brune, Agerholm and Liljas, 2023).

The media impact of COVID-19

If social media changed the face of news, COVID-19 changed the face of social media. With traditional media, particularly print, the message is usually one-way, at least most of the time: experts give their opinion and readers, listeners, or viewers receive the message passively. Where there are mechanisms for responses, they are usually carefully curated and time-limited.

With social media, however, the responses and queries are instantaneous and users generally expect to be able to engage with the originator of the information. Librarians can assist with the analysis of responses by suggesting tools including text mining, sentiment analysis and deep-learning models amongst others.

The use of social media during the pandemic further highlighted the importance of health literacy for the general public. In their scoping review (2022), Joseph et al. identified three major themes: sources of misinformation, impact of misinformation and strategies to limit misinformation. The remedy to this misinformation was found to be ensuring that misinformation was countered with evidence-based information and advice.

The use of behavioural theory in social media messaging

While the official channels and output were, presumably, in the main operating from a point of duty of care and consideration to keep citizens safe during the pandemic, psychological techniques were also used to achieve the result they desired. Although the 'Nudge Unit' of the UK government was established in 2010, it was employed to craft the government response to the COVID-19 outbreak, working in tandem with the Department of Health and Social Care.

Joseph et al. (2022) studied Facebook, Twitter, websites of some agencies and online newspaper sites in detail and discovered that most of the misinformation claims related to the illness itself. This included how it was transmitted, mortality rates, how it was under control, treatment and potential cures. While sentiment analysis, text mining and textual analysis techniques can be applied to public tweets and posts, it is much more difficult to analyse private messages on platforms such as WhatsApp, due to their privacy settings. When many of these messages were made available in the public interest as part of the enquiry into the English government's handling of the pandemic, the strained relationships between some of the major players were all too apparent (Seddon, 2023).

Of the 'open' social media networks, YouTube and Facebook were the two platforms with the highest levels of users holding conspiracy theory beliefs. Younger users were more likely to believe, endorse and forward those theories. For YouTube, over 25% of the most viewed videos in English incorporated information that was non-factual or misleading. The more likely users were to believe in conspiracy theories, the less likely they were to follow behaviours designed for health protection.

Joseph et al. (2022) described a twofold approach to misinformation, with mobile instant messages requiring a 'micro-level' approach and television and radio broadcasts, magazines and newspapers requiring a 'macro-level' option. Other notable examples of potentially lethal misinformation included the 45th US President's endorsement of hydroxychloroquine as a cure and a general conspiracy theory about microchips in vaccines (Dow et al., 2021).

The infodemic

Part of the issue around the severity of misinformation relating to the COVID-19 pandemic as it manifested on social media is likely to lie with the sheer volume of information produced during the pandemic, which was quite startling. At the time of writing, in early autumn 2024, PubMed alone had over 438,245 papers listed with COVID as a keyword. In total, 362,828 of those were published during the official time frame of the outbreak as declared by the WHO, from 11 March 2020 to 5 May 2023.

This immense amount of information has often been described as an 'infodemic'. According to the Merriam-Webster dictionary, this word was coined in 2003 by David Rothkopf in the *Washington Post* in relation to SARS. This outbreak of severe acute respiratory syndrome was less widespread than COVID-19, affecting only 30 countries, with China and Hong Kong hardest hit.

Responsible use of social media facilitates access to information for the public relating to new developments, discoveries made by scientists, guidelines and potential interventions, remedies and vaccine progress. It also allows a global view. In this respect, however, one of the major strengths of social media, namely the fact that anyone can create and disseminate content, can become a weakness. With the 'novel' nature of the coronavirus (novel meaning 'new'), there was a great deal of fear and apprehension, with the result that many people grabbed whatever information they could find.

As the pandemic continued, the 'infodemic' began to take a turn towards misinformation with serious implications, often described as 'fake news'. Social media also lends itself only too easily to those whose motives may not have the best interest of their audience at heart. Social media posts often relate to entertainment, self-promotion, or the originator becoming a self-declared 'influencer'. In addition, the algorithms that sit behind social media platforms recommend content to users that is similar to what has already been viewed. While the mainstream media was often far from blameless in its approach to delivering information that was less than evidence-based, social media was frequently instrumental in spreading sensationalised and inaccurate information.

Sensationalism and conspiracy theories

Joseph et al. (2022) have observed that in times of disaster and emergency, this tendency to sensationalism gets worse. Indeed, it often results in both conspiracy theories and lowered trust in the health officials, workers and others who are doing their best to protect and inform the public. The impact of this spread of misinformation can be shown to have a direct impact on levels of mental health.

One of the conspiracy rumours of the time included the position that COVID-19 was spread by the 5G mobile network, or that other common over-the-counter medications such as ibuprofen could increase the chances of COVID-19 infection.

Borges do Nascimento et al. (2022) have identified several potentially negative consequences of misinformation around health, including misleading or downright incorrect interpretations of the evidence available. Other negative consequences were mental health impacts, health resources being misallocated and an increase in hesitancy around vaccinations. They concluded that infodemics in health emergencies result in adverse effects on society.

This misinformation made it more difficult for public health officials to get the message out about preventative measures such as masks, social distancing and, once available, vaccinations. Meanwhile, suggestions of dubious 'cures' proliferated, from drinking cow urine and hot water to ingesting chlorine.

Attempts to combat COVID-19 misinformation

Given the importance of images on social media, the WHO attempted to combat the torrent of misinformation by sharing infographics about various aspects of the disease but in some cases it was too late. Joseph et al. (2022) suggest some ways to combat the spread of conspiracy theories, for example taking down accounts set up deliberately to spread incorrect information. Influencers are another group that could have been recruited to assist, particularly if they were trusted public figures with a sufficient following. The key was to spread evidence-based information on the same platform where the misinformation was spread. As information professionals, we can help analyse the context of any 'fake news' along with attempting to uncover the reasons for the spread. This might include the type of account, whether it belongs to a group, individual, or even an official outlet. In addition, the tone of the tweet or post could be analysed, as well as whether there is any evidence to support the 'fake news'. As in so many situations, Joseph et al. (2022) found the terms used were vital, with 'corona' resulting in the highest levels of information that was unverifiable. By contrast, 'COVID-19' and the hashtag '#coronavirusoutbreak' were at the other end of the scale.

Other aspects of the virus that were questioned included the origin and seriousness of the virus and in some cases governments themselves were not exempt from spreading misinformation. Russian campaigns, for example, were highlighted in this respect (Jaeger and Taylor, 2021), with some other governments censoring the information available to citizens. Bramstedt (2020) is one of those who has pointed out how the rush to publish research during the COVID-19 pandemic led to peer review processes that were compromised, with some of the research published being substandard.

The effect of the pandemic on libraries

The pandemic, or specifically the lockdowns that accompanied it, had an extremely disruptive effect on many aspects of everyday life, including library provision. Libraries pivoted to find new ways to meet user needs during the pandemic and those whose responsibilities included providing literature searches often found themselves producing rapid literature reviews and searching for topics that were new to their experience. This was against a backdrop of a severe dearth of publications in the early days and a surfeit of publications as the pandemic progressed.

While misinformation and disinformation are two of the terms often used, other terms that can help identify misleading information include pseudohistorical or pseudoscientific.

The role of librarians in uncovering COVID-19 research

Librarians also had to come up with innovative ways to uncover research on COVID-19 until, and even after, the term itself was added to the official list of MeSH headings on 7 July 2020. Search strategies had to be adapted and around the world there were repositories built of expert searches focused on the topic (Gorring et al., 2022). Suggested approaches to combat the 'fake news' epidemic that accompanied the physical pandemic included working in partnership with other partners beyond the usually suggested health professionals. Suggestions for future collaborations included journalism or media professionals, community organisations and public libraries. As discussed earlier in the chapter on health research, one aspect of healthcare research to be on guard for is papers that have been retracted. Where it concerns COVID-19, one of the highest profile was the interesting case of Surgisphere, discussed a little later.

We also need to be alert to the way in which information is organised, whether it is generated by AI and understand what cues to look for to identify misinformation. Finally, there were some papers that stated or suggested that librarians had an obligation or imperative to combat misinformation, whether that be a professional, moral or ethical obligation (Young et al., 2020; Herrero-Diz and López-Rufino, 2021). These papers used terms like 'should' or 'must', in contrast to some of the other papers who suggested ideas, using language like 'well positioned to create solutions' or 'we see an opportunity for'.

There are many strategies here that health libraries could implement to address misinformation. However, authors have generally not addressed considerations of feasibility for health libraries given their limited resources, nor what is reasonable given the goals of parent organisations. For example, collaborations with external organisations or providing resources and training externally might be possible in an academic setting but outside the scope of librarians working in a hospital. Health librarians must carefully consider what is practicable in their own context.

Based on this review, identifying predatory journals (Herrero-Diz and López-Rufino, 2021), identifying misinformation via checklists such as creating blacklists and whitelists – e.g. Beall's list and contributions to DOAJ (Krawczyk and Kulczycki, 2021) – were major health library activities.

COVID misinformation: the curious case of Surgisphere

In 2020, in the early days of the COVID-19 pandemic, a tiny US company called Surgisphere claimed to have huge amounts of data concerning patients who had contracted this novel disease. The company was founded in 2008 by Sapan Desai and started life as a textbook marketing company before transitioning into data analytics. The company came under intense scrutiny when it provided large datasets of COVID-19 patients to researchers. The data was subsequently used in studies published in some of the most prestigious medical journals in the world.

Despite the fact that the company had barely any employees and only the scantiest of social media and web presences, *The New England Journal of Medicine* and *The Lancet* were amongst the eminent journals that published papers based on the supposed data. While social media may have been one of the main methods of distribution of misinformation around the topic, it was also on social media that the data was ultimately called out (Buck, 2020).

Some studies claimed that hydroxychloroquine, a drug touted as a potential COVID-19 treatment, significantly increased the risk of death. When a subsequent death occurred which was attributed to the 'wrongful ingestion of a chloroquine-containing compound', the scene was set for a massive investigation and subsequent scandal.

The publicity around hydroxychloroquine was heightened by the apparent endorsement of the substance as a cure by the 45th US President Donald J.

Trump, one of the most influential individuals in the world, with a massive following on social media.

In their study, Niburski and Niburski (2020) found that the then President of the United States made 11 tweets between 1 March and 30 April 2020 on the topic of COVID-19 therapies that were unproven. Using data extracted from White House briefings, the research also found that he mentioned these 65 times. Amazon data showed that following the President's first press conference on 19 March 2020 and subsequent tweets on 21 March 2020, Amazon purchases for medicine substitutes including hydroxychloroquine increased by 200%.

At the time of writing, Surgisphere no longer exists as a functional company. Following the massive scandal involving the fraudulent data used in their studies, the reputation of the company was irreparably damaged. The company website was taken down and any remnants of their online presence were erased. The incident serves as a stark reminder of the importance of rigorous data verification in scientific research.

Misleading healthcare information on social media platforms

When Wojtara (2023) carried out a review of social media in dermatology education, it highlighted several platforms that carried information that was not only misleading but, in some cases, dangerous. YouTube, TikTok, Instagram and Reddit were mentioned most often, with one notable feature across all platforms: the lack of qualified clinicians posting.

The slight ambivalence around the use of social media as a potential information and education dissemination channel was also particularly apparent in the early days of the pandemic. Ng and Indran (2023) identified how slow, in general, scholars have been to pick up on the trend for older content creators to contribute to social media channels. They also discovered that twice as many videos on TikTok were created by women compared to men.

The COVID-19 pandemic highlighted the importance of the need for reliable information, particularly around epidemiology and vaccines. TikTok in particular has been highlighted in many studies, due to its popularity with a group generally regarded as highly impressionable. The study of content relating to vaccines carried out by van Kampen et al. (2022) highlighted the need to incorporate new social media platforms into medical education, as a method of ensuring trainees' readiness to engage with patients on what they call 'novel platforms'. Posts and videos around many other conditions have been shown to be equally misleading. For attention deficit/hyperactivity disorder (ADHD), for instance, one of the most popular topics in healthcare on TikTok, Yeung, Ng and Abi-Jaoude (2022) identified that many of the most popular 100 videos could be classified as misleading or personal experience.

Besides the specific case of COVID-19, there is a history of misinformation and sensationalisation related to healthcare on social media. Other subsequent examples include monkeypox (Edinger et al., 2023; Meyer et al., 2023).

For librarians, finding quality assessment tools that can help identify, analyse and counter misinformation is one of the most useful roles that can be assumed.

Information inequality

There is also an element of information provision that appears to have been discussed only rarely, which is the role of information inequality in being able to access robust evidence sources. This circumstance appeared to mean that members of the general public were more prone to believing conspiracy theories and social media posts rife with misinformation (Herrero-Diz and López-Rufino, 2021). Alternative or complementary therapies with little supporting evidence may also be recommended on social media – despite the lack of robust support in the literature or research (Bianchini et al., 2019).

Countering misinformation on social media with quality assessment

Quality assessment of content on social media is also a concern for Li et al. (2024), who used a range of quality evaluation tools. Their approach incorporated DISCERN, PEMAT (A/V), GQS, JAMA, HONcode and other specialised instruments. One notable disadvantage of using these, however, is that they were not developed to assess short videos related to health science, although doctors and medical students were amongst the experts who assessed the content and quality.

While social media is often used as a mode of spreading misinformation, healthcare information professionals can help track down accurate, robustly evidence-based information backed up by research. While COVID-19 and the sheer volume of misinformation produced and disseminated during the pandemic is an especially stark case, it also holds lessons for the future for all of us around blind belief without checking the facts and, where necessary, applying a liberal dose of scepticism.

Ultimately, whatever the media channel, misinformation is misinformation. The risk with social media is that it is so accessible for so many people. In the 1980s there was a tendency for consumers to believe the statement 'I read it in the newspaper so it must be true', in the 2020s, in many cases, this appears to have metamorphosed into 'I read/saw it on social media so it must be true'.

CHAPTER 7

Barriers to the Use of Social Media in Healthcare Settings

Introduction

In recent years there have been many acknowledgements of the importance of the online world if we are to advance our knowledge of healthcare information and help patients access robust evidence-based resources, but this brave new world is riddled with barriers. Some of these barriers are technological; others related to skills mix; while still others relate to finances.

Although there are often basic free versions of social media apps available, one issue with these is that they may often come with advertising and sponsorship which may not always be appropriate to healthcare settings. Where sites make heavy use of modern technology or popups these are often blocked, leading to a suboptimal experience for users.

Other barriers to the use of technology in general and social media in particular, include low network speeds; copyright and intellectual property; commercial in confidence data; data protection; lack of training for librarians and others who put social media sites together; and, in some cases, technophobia.

Unfortunately, despite several published strategies outlining the importance of technology, including the NHS *Long Term Workforce Plan* (NHS England, 2023b), many NHS and public sector institutions in particular remain suspicious of and even hostile to the whole idea of social media. The situation has not been helped by some recent high-profile security lapses and cyberattacks which often either target patient data directly, as in the 2017 WannaCry attack, or bring systems crashing to a halt, as in the 2024 CrowdStrike incident.

In addition, most healthcare libraries or units are constantly having to justify their budgets while still finding a way to fulfil their contract with their host and overarching organisations. For charities, non-profits and commercial organisations, access is rather more of a mix, although there too, libraries and information services are often constantly under threat. Commercial companies may find themselves battling situations around commercial in confidence data and/or intellectual property.

Overcoming barriers: proving the impact of social media

Elliott (2014) has also identified some of the unique challenges that hospital librarians face when they are trying to launch social media accounts to support their service. These include staff changes, concerns around privacy and consent and differing perceptions of what the purpose of social media may be. A further barrier which has become more important in recent years is the need to prove the impact of social media, which is somewhat time-consuming.

Gaps in the literature around the use of social media in health information settings

Elliott (2014) identified a gap in the literature on the use of social media in health information settings. The gap was clearly evident around the lack of research into the ways in which hospital librarians can navigate the structures of organisations to implement social media accounts, particularly new ones.

The research identified how rarely hospital librarians have complete autonomy over any efforts they might make to implement their online outreach efforts. Elliott's literature review unveiled several common barriers to the effective use of social media, from privacy and security consents to varying perceptions of the purpose of social media, along with the occasional reluctance of library staff to move into the new roles incorporating social media management.

Elliott (2014) also identified that some of the resistance librarians typically met with regards to the implementation of social media came from the IT departments along with marketing and legal departments. In later years marketing has often been subsumed into communication and legal may work alongside or have been incorporated into information governance.

Hospital librarians attempting to add social media to their libraries' outreach efforts often meet resistance from information technology (IT), marketing and legal departments. By anticipating and planning for these organisational barriers, librarians can present a strong case for launching and maintaining new library social media accounts (Lafferty, 2013).

Linguistic barriers and health literacy

Health information is notoriously complex, especially when we take into account that almost half of the adult population of England (43%) struggles to merely read, let alone understand health information. Simultaneously, understanding many aspects of healthcare now relies on not only high levels of literacy, but high levels of internet competence as well.

While it is difficult enough for many users to understand text-based information, when numeracy or dosages are added to the mix, the low levels of numeracy in the general population are even more startlingly high – 61%. Librarians can play a pivotal role in helping to tackle these gaps by working with other communities and healthcare professionals from other sectors, effectively forming compacts to assess the best way to create sustainable approaches to increasing both digital literacy and ultimately, general levels of health.

The language around the use of technology and social media can be a barrier in itself, particularly when librarians are attempting to understand why users do – or don't – opt for social media platforms in their information seeking. Ebenezer (2017) found, for instance, that Web 2.0 was little understood as a term, but social media enjoyed slightly more recognition.

One of the barriers to the effective use of social media is what Wojtara (2023) refers to as 'complex and often technical verbiage'. Morse et al. (2024) also identify the readability, or lack of readability, of posts on social media as a barrier in otolaryngologic diagnoses. In general, posts made by laypeople were more readable than posts made by medical professionals.

Digital inequality

Digital inequality is another potential barrier to accessing healthcare information that is currently attracting a good deal of attention in the NHS in particular. It's something of a paradox that some NHS healthcare organisations communicate with their patients and service users via social media, but do not extend the same privileges to their staff.

Where some Trusts have policies encouraging their employees 'to use social media in a confident coherent way' (Fitzgerald, 2019) or to use social media 'to share best practice, as a tool for discovering best practice and to check for important updates or news from the Trust' (Moreman, 2020), at some other Trusts, where social media is not blocked entirely, it may only be available to employees at particular times of day, for instance between 12 noon and 2 p.m. or after 6 p.m. (Fraser, 2021). Some Trusts require a justification for access to social media endorsed by a senior manager and some patient-facing organisations restrict access to particular members of staff (Aspiro Healthcare, 2015).

For those working in academic or commercial organisations, access to social media may be more open, although this depends on the organisation.

Facebook algorithms and changes to the platforms

Policy changes

Even if today's most popular social media platforms, such as Facebook and TikTok, continue to grow and increase numbers of users, it's inevitable that site policies will change, often in response to legislation or new technologies that arise. The other aspect of social media platforms that librarians need to consider is that the behind-the-scenes algorithms that dictate, to a large extent, what we see will continue to evolve or mutate. In this respect we are at the mercy of the platform owners, most of whom are focused on profits or at the least commodifying users.

Just over ten years ago, in late 2013, Facebook gave a glimpse of our current social media landscape when their newsfeed algorithm was changed to give greater prominence to what the algorithm deemed most relevant. As a result, brand pages were displayed differently; users who had 'liked' brand pages no longer saw every update or post from the brand. Ultimately, we are all subject to the control of the social media owners.

Regular changes to platforms can also make it more difficult for healthcare librarians to consistently monitor trends in usage and engagement, as well as making it harder to compare these aspects year on year. In addition, as new iterations of social media platforms appear, it can be difficult if not impossible for librarians to obtain clearance for what is often regarded as new software by computing departments. Working with communications teams, education teams, information governance and computing departments may be helpful in this respect, but there are no guarantees of consistency.

Hashtags

One way to attempt to combat the ever-changing algorithm is to adapt our search techniques, including the use of hashtags to track what is happening in a particular area. Hashtags, effectively keywords or phrases describing the content in a pithy, concise way, marked with the hash sign often used to denote a number, offer one way to help users decide what themes to follow (Thelwall and Thelwall, 2020). Hashtags also help social media users understand what is transpiring, healthwise, all over the world in the fastest way possible. Hashtags can ensure that the status of the situation is communicated very rapidly (Naeem and Bhatti, 2020). Once again, Facebook,

WhatsApp, Twitter (X) and Instagram are particularly popular, although not all make use of hashtags.

Metadata, or data about data, describes various aspects of social media posts, including who authored the post, the message type, the date and time of the post, links, as well as the location, comments and likes. Hashtags are a type of metadata, particularly on Twitter (X) and Instagram, prefaced by the hash symbol '#'. Hashtags work as a kind of short description or keyword outlining what the post is about and offer a way to cross-reference content by theme or topic. It's also possible to search Instagram or Twitter (X) for hashtags to retrieve all the posts tagged with that term or set of keywords. Hashtags may incorporate letters, numerals, or some special characters such as underscores.

Back in 2007, Chris Messina was an American blogger who first proposed the use of what came to be called hashtags. Messina did not patent the term, but hashtags became a feature of Twitter and subsequently Facebook, YouTube and Instagram. These keywords or short phrases both describe the content of a post and enable users to search for connected posts. In 2014, the word 'hashtag' was incorporated into the *Oxford English Dictionary*. There is a current limit of 30 hashtags on a social media post on Instagram, although advice in general is to stick to three to five tags (Gotter, 2024).

The Healthcare Hashtag Project

Over the years there have been several attempts to improve accessibility of information, including the Healthcare Hashtag Project. This project was designed with the intention of simplifying and organising the wide range of hashtags on Twitter related to healthcare. This was in an effort to combat one of the barriers to using the internet in general, namely finding the information we need in the first place.

The project was created to make it easier for healthcare professionals, patients and caregivers to find relevant conversations and communities on social media. Key features included categorising hashtags into groups by topic and frequency of use; the identification of what we now know as influencers, highlighting key individuals in specific areas of healthcare; and real-time monitoring, in which it was possible to follow a live feed of conversations related to specific hashtags. This approach is often used to effectively broadcast conferences, for example. This attempt to consolidate and standardise healthcare hashtags had the ultimate aim of improving the accessibility and effectiveness of social media for the wider healthcare community.

The Healthcare Hashtag Project has been widely regarded as a success, resulting in significant improvements to the way healthcare professionals, patients and caregivers interacted on social media. The Healthcare Hashtag Project captured over 100 million tweets on health topics. Along with the enhanced discoverability of relevant conversations and communities, the project resulted in improved efficiency, as time spent searching for relevant hashtags was reduced, along with increased engagement from the healthcare community. The platform also provided insights into hashtag usage and trends.

Social media: considering the audience

Some healthcare information professionals may find themselves creating social media posts aimed at patients or even caregivers and, along with the content and suitability of language used, there are issues around privacy and patient confidentiality to consider.

Diversity issues are also likely to be a factor in what social media is used and how. Librarians need to consider whether the audience will be mostly patients and whether those patients are likely to be most interested in a particular health condition or concern. Before launching a social media campaign, healthcare information professionals are likely to find it very beneficial to run a pre-launch survey. As librarians and healthcare professionals know only too well, however, it's wise to be as responsive as possible to changes in direction from the organisation, national bodies or social media users themselves.

Stylesheets and consistent approaches to social media also help the library service to present a coherent image to library users and making use of scheduling software like Feedly or TweetDeck can also help to take the pressure off colleagues. Setting up a social media calendar, making use of additional tools like the *Calendar of National Campaigns* published by NHS Employers can also help with planning (NHS Employers, 2025). Other sources include the World Health Organization (WHO, n.d.) and Awareness Days (National Awareness Days, 2024).

All of this can help combat the potential barrier to using social media which staff changes or rotations pose, but diplomacy and creativity will often be necessary to persuade organisations to allow libraries and information services to incorporate social media into their workstreams effectively.

Communications guidelines

While in some cases hospital librarians may, historically, have been able to exercise control and independence over their approach to social media, in others the communications and/or marketing department exercises high levels of editorial control. Social media leaves organisations exposed to criticism, meaning that library managers and directors may need to get buy-in from comms as well as other parts of the organisations.

Another barrier is uncertainty around the purpose of social media in the first place. A regular challenge for hospital librarians is having to explain that knowledge and information services have a purpose far beyond giving out resources. Those healthcare information professionals who wish to focus on sharing information and connecting with their users online need to emphasise that this is the main purpose of their use of social media.

Trending hashtags and topics on social media don't always present content that is informational, as can be seen from campaigns like the #IceBucketChallenge, which raised awareness of amyotrophic lateral sclerosis (ALS). Both celebrities and members of the general public shared videos that challenged followers and/or friends to make a donation to the ALS Association. Although the challenge raised levels of general awareness about the condition and helped to attract financial donations, those who required information needed to search for it on their own. Hospital and other healthcare librarians may be able to use this as a blueprint for recognising similar opportunities to add informational resources to topics that are trending. It could also be constructive for social media roles to be modelled on the approaches of large non-profit organisations. A content analysis of tweets from 73 of the largest 100 US non-profits uncovered the fact that just under 59% had given information as their focus. A further 25.8% focused on building relationships and community, a type of tweet that was valuable for marketing purposes, but most of all useful for building both trust in and understanding of organisations.

Few health librarians are able to operate with complete independence when it comes to the outreach messages and efforts of their service; it's almost always necessary to consider challenges and expectations from within their own organisations. Those healthcare information professionals who plan implementable ways to protect privacy of both healthcare professionals and users on social media may meet with organisational support.

Healthcare information professionals also need to be primed to respond to the regular, almost continuous changes that occur on proprietary social platforms if they are hoping to meet with success in both launching new accounts and growing online audiences.

Staffing considerations

A further barrier to the use of social media in healthcare information is presented by the challenges facing healthcare libraries around the world in terms of closures and consequent reductions in staffing levels (Harrow et al., 2019). One possible countermeasure may be found in the more personalised approach outlined by Williams (2022). As staffing levels in healthcare libraries continue to fall and physical spaces continue to be encroached upon, however (Grabeel, Watson and Wilson, 2023), healthcare information professionals will need to take a judiciously targeted approach, particularly in educational settings (Li et al., 2019). In extreme cases, services are being closed down entirely (Harrow et al., 2019).

Amongst the various approaches that may need to be investigated include what Morgan (2019) describes as contingency librarians or Just's (2003) outline of sharing staff between hospital and academic libraries. Although there are clear suggestions around the ratio of qualified staff numbers to the populations they serve, at least in the NHS, there remain significant differences between regions, despite Topol Review recommendations (Health Education England, 2019).

Skills training for library staff is another potential barrier to the implementation of social media, both in terms of time and cost, as well as the frustrations that often accompany the technological barriers to the use of social media in healthcare information settings.

Those in charge of a service may also need to consider rearranging staff roles to include responsibility for posting on social media, ensuring that there is clarity around the purpose of that use of social media.

The skills gap and CPD

Social media also offers healthcare information professionals the opportunity to attend or present at conferences overseas without leaving their own desktop. Attendees at conferences frequently share their experiences in the form of blog posts or tweets, allowing their peers to share the experience and providing a 'stream of consciousness' reflective mini CPD experience for themselves. In addition, social media platforms in the form of LibraryThing have offered librarians the chance to collaborate on projects such as the 2021–2023 updates of the Core Collections of suggested titles for nursing, medical and mental health libraries.

Vimeo, YouTube, SlideShare and others offer the option to share research, potentially both widening access to a global audience and acting as a cost-effective and accessible repository.

Changing staff roles

Another potential staff-related barrier to the successful implementation and use of social media can arise where staff transition roles or acquire additional duties and responsibilities. Although librarians are skilled at juggling roles and responsibilities and as rewarding as social media can be, managing it can be very time-consuming, particularly in small teams. In some cases, especially where staffing is constrained, librarians may find themselves having to present a strategy to senior managers or stakeholders. One suggested approach from Fernandez (2009) is to incorporate a SWOT analysis, as this is one way to ensure that social media audiences are taken into account. Healthcare information professionals are also likely to find it useful to understand their own skills and those of their teams, as Waddell, Barnes and Khan-Kernahan (2012) have emphasised.

Lack of time

Early adopter Giustini outlined in 2014 how time is often a barrier for health librarians wanting to incorporate social media into their practice. For him, two of the main purposes of social media were lifelong learning and promotion of the profession.

Security considerations

In recent years, there have been issues around the security of computer systems and networks in hospital settings, including the WannaCry ransomware attack in 2017. The increased vigilance and security measures that need to be put in place can often result in additional issues around being able to access online resources.

While the blocking of malicious content as defined by NHS Digital is an unarguable necessity (NHS Digital, 2022) particularly in the light of recent cyberattacks, what is less comprehensible is the blocking of educational content. In some cases, this even includes content on NHS England's own YouTube channels that is referenced in national e-learning courses. Increasingly, e-books, social media and cloud computing access are required to allow medical, nursing, allied health and healthcare students to access resources essential for their studies and yet these too can be blocked. Google Drive is a particular target for IT departments in some parts of the country and in some cases even organisational OneDrive access is blocked by some NHS IT departments.

While some IT departments have now accepted the necessity of Microsoft Teams as a communication platform with reluctance, despite evidence that it is a useful tool which can bring about efficiencies (Lawson et al., 2023), some other commonly used apps such as Zoom are not endorsed, following alarm around security concerns (Soni, 2020). Skype, meanwhile, despite being another Microsoft product similar to Teams, has continued to lose market share following repeated revamps. Although there are still over 8,000 Skype users in the UK, this is far behind the USA, with over 38,500 users (Elad, 2024). These Skype usage figures fade into insignificance compared to the 300 million plus users for Microsoft Teams, which is endorsed for use within the NHS (Curry, 2025).

In the spring budget of 2024, funding was announced to the tune of £3.4 billion for NHS technology with a view to driving improvements in productivity that could support the NHS Long Term Workforce Plan, starting in spring 2025. While the focus on technology – and the funding – is welcome and very much needed, the jury remains out on whether this will translate into concrete improvements and outcomes beneficial to patients. As recently as 2023, the progress made by the UK government in areas of digital transformation was rated as 'inadequate'. The research highlighted areas that have a detrimental effect on productivity. Laptops may lack adequate battery life; 22% of doctors described their IT systems as 'not fit for purpose'; and an estimated 8% of GP time was lost to IT issues.

Talking about a world where the NHS is 'AI-ready' does not take into account the fact that in some organisations, social media remains blocked, let alone AI. The aspirations of the 2019 Topol Review are that technology could release time to allow clinicians to provide care. Unfortunately, the timing of the review, just before the pandemic, means that in some healthcare information environments, this goal seems lofty and somewhat remote. The aspiration to implement technology also fails to take into account the differing organisational cultures often within the same organisation. Where digital staff passports, for example, may hold the potential to improve flexible working, the probability is that not all staff will be able to reap the benefits in the same way.

There is at present an understandable emphasis on the need for productivity, although even the amount of funding announced is likely to merely touch the sides in improving this – and that is assuming that the funding can be protected for its intended spending on digital technology and transformation. The NHS has a 'history of raiding capital budgets to prop up day-to-day costs' while simultaneously 'underspending on technology'.

In addition, NHS transformation projects can often suffer from 'short-term and rushed' funding and a final potential staff side barrier to consider is that staff need the skills to make best use of technology and the time to acquire them (Mistry, 2024).

While most larger cities in England benefit from robust internet, via high capacity bandwidth and/or Wi-Fi signals, this is not the case everywhere. In fact, at least a quarter of the UK is highly likely to find accessing online services something of a struggle.

There are also some notable exceptions in the budget, particularly social care. Again, while partnership is a stated aim, in practice some parts of the healthcare system are likely to inevitably lag behind (Mistry, Lindsay and Patterson, 2024).

Cyberattacks

While they do not only impact social media, cyberattacks and even systems failures can have a devastating effect on the entire information infrastructure. In summer 2024, numerous systems around the world experienced a complete technical breakdown due to an update in CrowdStrike (EC-Council, 2024). General practitioners in particular who found their work impacted described a system that was no 'longer fit for purpose' (Guyoncourt, 2024b). The Royal College of General Practitioners (RCGP) were also clear in their concerns, citing 'decades of underfunding' and systems that were 'slow, out of date and inflexible' (Guyoncourt, 2024b). There are currently two main patient record systems in primary care, EMIS and SystmOne.

While built-in obsolescence appears to be a feature of many, if not all, technologies and as new software is developed and released, new hardware needs to be implemented. This does not appear to have been taken into account in many aspects of using technology in the healthcare system. In some cases, it can take as long as a minute for a page of patient information to load. The average consultation time with a GP is ten minutes (Gopfert et al., 2021).

Some NHS Trusts do not permit staff access to social media sites such as Facebook and Twitter during working hours, unless authorised for specific business purposes (Fraser, 2021). Healthcare information on social media is notoriously vulnerable to phishing, a particular method of harvesting personal information using e-mail or messaging (Priestman et al., 2019). With this as the backdrop, it is easy to understand the reluctance of many healthcare practitioners to even contemplate using social media, despite the potential benefits.

Technological barriers

There can sometimes be a perception amongst decision makers and senior budget holders that technology is a universal panacea which will potentially mean fewer staff are required, although some commentators are more sanguine (Moulds and Horton, 2023).

One of the major barriers, however, to implementing social media remains technology, not just the availability – or lack – of technology, but its rapid revolution. Social media platforms themselves, let alone the content they contain, have shown themselves to be less than future-proof. In some cases new sites were built over the old foundations of defunct or even obsolete social media sites. Sites like MySpace, Google Wave and Friendster are now almost forgotten and hospital librarians and others wishing to incorporate social media into their service successfully need to ensure there are plans in place to adopt and adapt if necessary. The length of these plans may be as short as a few months or as long as five years.

Even before the pandemic, the Topol Review (Health Education England, 2019) had identified several technologies that were likely to have a major impact on future patient care, including digital medicine and AI, various telemedicine apps, including remote diagnosis and monitoring biosensors and smartphone apps. Many clinicians and librarians are forced to circumvent limited access to applications other than those provided via Microsoft if the signal is robust enough, by using their own smartphones or tablets to access data and carry out daily tasks. Kraushaar and Bohnet-Joschko (2023) found that more junior physicians were more likely to use their phones in this way.

Although the technological ambitions for the use of technology in the workplace are laudable, even essential, if the UK healthcare system is to keep pace with progress around the world, it was apparent even in the early days of social media that lack of access to robust technology might be something of an issue, in hospital settings in particular. In fact, these promising new techniques and ways of working posed a particular issue for those with a joint HE/NHS role with the lack of access on NHS computers described as 'generally problematic' (Lafferty, 2013). It was also observed in the same study that 'many NHS organisations also limit and or restrict access to many social media and Web 2.0 technology websites'.

In some cases, users were able to bypass this by bringing in their own devices but this relies on robust Wi-Fi or mobile signals, which can often be problematic in hospital settings (Sheerer, 2024). In terms of barriers to use, this area is relatively little discussed in the literature, but in some settings the connectivity, or IT department's reluctance, fear or lack of skills and knowledge can result in it being extremely difficult to access these resources for patient care, no matter how useful they may be.

The growing role of technology in healthcare has been highlighted for well over a decade, since a new strategy issued by the Department of Health in 2012 (Department of Health, 2012). Despite this central encouragement and policies encouraging the move towards incorporating online technologies into healthcare practice, there was awareness even then that 'permission to embrace digital opportunities in the NHS is typically heavily restricted'. The resultant frustration on the part of many users was acknowledged (Ebenezer, 2017), particularly where users had both NHS and Higher Education affiliations.

Despite the fact that the internet is, in most cases, now embedded in our workflows, there remain some healthcare information environments where barriers to the use of social media and indeed technology in general remain, particularly in some pockets of the NHS. In general, Higher Education institutions were a long way ahead, and still are, in adopting new technologies, compared to the NHS, public libraries or some other sectors.

Over ten years after Lafferty highlighted this as an issue (2013), in some cases the situation has not improved. Particularly in the NHS, organisations may have their own Twitter, Facebook, YouTube and other social media official sites blocked on the main computer network. As late as 2020, examples of organisations in this category included NHS Western Isles (Fraser, 2021). Librarians in healthcare settings often find themselves supporting e-learning, also known as online learning, internet-based learning and, sometimes, as Technology Enhanced Learning (TEL). Librarians may find themselves required as a guide to the vagaries and sometimes less than intuitive interfaces, or as content creators. Mahdavi Ardestani et al. (2023) found that many organisations have incorporated e-learning into their educational policies: on paper at least, it appears an attractive proposition. The majority of the learning can take place remotely, requiring only a smartphone and a live internet connection and from a cost-effectiveness perspective it is also enticing. This approach does, however, assume that all e-learning participants are sufficiently literate and IT-literate to be able to complete the learning without assistance, which is not always the case. The study does, however, acknowledge that there has always been 'frustration with technological issues among learners, leading to a need for related technological support'.

In 2019, when the NHS Long Term Plan was published, the ambition to incorporate 'digitally-enabled care' into mainstream healthcare was boldly stated. Various white papers followed and during the COVID pandemic, as is often the case in times of sudden upheaval, the use of technology solutions in NHS healthcare took a bold step forward. As well as the use of Microsoft Teams (mostly) for professional collaborations, video and online consultations increased dramatically. As a countermeasure to the misinformation rife on some areas of social media, trusted patient videos were made available to and via NHS clinical staff with no cost implications. Remote monitoring also became a feature of supporting patients and some aspects of information sharing improved.

Technological barriers: not just a UK issue

Technological barriers to the use of social media in healthcare information are not limited only to the UK; even in highly advanced countries like Sweden, where medical libraries are largely digitised, situations differ between libraries in academic and hospital settings and individual libraries. In an ideal world the Swedish model may be one to aspire to, with AI, smart technologies and big data all areas for development.

Despite the substantial possibilities of new technology for improved productivity and responsiveness, in order to be able to support healthcare professionals with moving towards this libraries need to be able to monitor new technologies, test them and ultimately adopt them.

The OECD has identified Sweden as highly advanced in both technological developments and digital services (OECD, 2018), with well-developed mobile and broadband networks. Besides this, there have been campaigns in Sweden to increase levels of digital literacy and medical libraries in Sweden have been at the forefront of adopting new technologies for at least the last decade (Ekstrand and Strandberg, 2023).

In Sweden, many libraries have high levels of autonomy, which is both a positive and a negative and has led to inequalities of resources in medical libraries. Although all colleges and universities are required to have a library, there is no equivalent requirement for the healthcare sector (Ranemo, 2022). The same division seen in the UK between academic and hospital libraries is therefore equally evident in Sweden. As in the UK, hospital libraries in Sweden are generally small, with fewer than ten staff, although unlike the UK, where medical library services are increasingly split across several sites, Swedish medical libraries are usually hosted by a single hospital site. Again as in the UK, conditions in hospital libraries are often very constrained, resulting in the necessity for collaboration, frequently including the use of Microsoft Teams or Zoom.

Several libraries had taken one step on from Web 2.0 or social media and were monitoring additional technologies like avatars, chatbots, drones and robotics. There were some areas of technology, however, including blockchain, biometrics and, to some extent, robotics that were only important to a small number of libraries.

There were notable differences between the sizes of libraries and the extent to which they were able to invest time in investigating and developing new technologies. Larger academic libraries were the ones with most staff and time resource to follow lines of investigations, while medium sized libraries usually adapted solutions already in existence. Smaller libraries had more difficulty in finding the time to work on projects and in general were less able to establish when they might be able to work on developments.

The high costs of providing electronic resources such as journals, e-books and point of care tools left very little if any flexibility to have the funds to spare for investigation of social media, Web 2.0 or Web 3.0 technologies.

In a parallel with British libraries, all hospital libraries in Sweden that took part in the study commented on how restrictive their IT environments were. It was generally not possible to install programs, for example and despite not dealing with patient data, library staff were subject to the same security restrictions as clinical professionals dealing with personal data. O'Doherty et al. (2018) also identified 'time constraints, poor technical skills, inadequate infrastructure, absence of institutional strategies and support and negative attitudes of all involved. Solutions to these include improved educator skills, incentives and reward for the time involved with development and delivery of online content, improved institutional strategies and support and positive attitude amongst all those involved in the development and delivery of online content.'

The ephemeral nature of social media

A further barrier to effective use of social media, and indeed the internet in general, in healthcare information lies in the ephemeral nature of the content and, in some cases, the platforms themselves. At the peak of its influence, it would have scarcely been imaginable that Twitter would find itself in the position it occupies, as the rebranded X, with a somewhat tarnished reputation and decreasing usage figures as well as some high-profile previous brands and individuals now abandoning X as a platform. Some platforms, such as Instagram, have embraced the temporary nature of social media into their fabric, with their 'stories' which expire after a specified time period. Whether social media itself is 'dying' remains a topic for debate, although some commentators believe so (Bogost, 2022) while others have identified that it is fragmenting rather than dying (Brandon, 2022).

In healthcare, one of the disciplines where decisions are based on historical developments and a body of evidence, this poses particularly thorny problems. Healthcare information professionals can assist in finding solutions to retrieve data, whether it involves the Wayback Machine, national or global union catalogues such as WorldCat or JISC Library Hub Discover (formerly COPAC), or the various regionally federated library management systems of the NHS.

Unfortunately, however, some of these are a little 'hit-and-miss' and vulnerable to the collection policy decisions of those running the servers with regard to what is available. GeoCities, mentioned in an earlier chapter, for example, disappeared for a short time until it was brought back via the

Wayback Machine. It's worth noting, however, that the Wayback Machine is blocked by many UK mobile network providers.

Grey or gray literature, taking the form of reports, conference proceedings and other lesser-known formats is also notoriously prone to disappearing and referencing such literature can be difficult. Social media is even more ephemeral, making it a difficult source to reference. In this book, a deliberate choice was made to reference academic sources where possible, based on the theory (rightly or wrongly) that they are less likely to disappear and more likely to be recoverable if they do vanish.

Librarians understand the need for information security and the resultant requirement for restrictions, but the impacts on professional information seeking can be difficult to live with. Librarians are not the only ones who have called into question the antipathy to social media in some areas. Ventola (2014a) has also highlighted the resistance to social media in healthcare settings.

Questions that are of particular interest include the reasons for the restrictions in the first place and whether there are any workarounds. In practice, many healthcare professionals and healthcare information professionals end up using their own devices with the attendant risks that this approach can bring (Glenton et al., 2024; Fenwick, 2014). The risks include the higher possibility of a breach of confidentiality – in terms of both patient data and 'commercial in confidence' information. Other risks may include concerns around professional reputation.

Breach of privacy is of particular concern where cameras are used. In one extreme case, an operation was live streamed accidentally on TikTok, later making its way to Twitter (Malhotra, 2023). This transfer of content between platforms, sometimes due to an automated process and sometimes unintentionally, is not uncommon; in fact there is some software that automatically updates more than one social channel at a time.

When the social media content produced originates from NHS organisations like NHS England or affiliated organisations such as the UK Health Security Association, finding the content difficult to access from within NHS Trusts can be even more frustrating. This is particularly the case where the originating organisations do not face the same restrictions themselves.

Fighting against these barriers can also be more time-consuming than it needs to be with time wasting and distractions potentially leading to errors, and cyberbullying another potentially troublesome area that requires careful management (Cain, Linos and Chretien 2019). Progress has been sporadic over the last two to three decades. Blenkinsopp (2008) outlines how the blocking of websites led to a survey overseen by the Strategic Health Authority Library Leads' (SHALL) Technical Design and Authority Group (TDAG) in which 151 NHS librarians were surveyed.

Issues around barriers to access to learning resources for junior doctors was investigated by Prince, Cass and Klaber (2010). These authors undertook a survey within 37 NHS Trusts of accessibility of web-based resources to postgraduate medical trainees. In each Trust a doctor on a computer within a clinical area tested access to a sample of 22 different online resources, including Web 2.0 and social media applications. They found that online video and audio (podcast) content was often difficult to view and sound was usually absent. YouTube was blocked in most Trusts and iTunes University was not accessible, as it requires iTunes to be installed.

In the case of education, while podcasts offered a promising option, they could not always be downloaded successfully in hospital settings due to the insufficient bandwidth of the network. In addition, social media was frequently thought of as being high-risk where confidentiality was concerned. Nurses in particular expressed concern with respect to confidentiality, with additional dismissal of social media as time-consuming or trivial or at best of no interest. In the early days of social media in particular, there were evident wide generational differences in both use and expectations, with some research respondents describing the lack of access to file storage such as Dropbox as a hindrance to working collaboratively.

YouTube, interestingly, was highlighted early on as a potentially very useful platform and resource where education was concerned. As usage increased, organisational policies around usage also increased and it would be a very rare organisation indeed in the mid-2020s that did not have a formal policy in place.

Despite initiatives by NHS England (2023a, 2023b) to promote the wider use of social media, their use within corporate networks continues to be tightly regulated. Increasingly widespread corporate use by NHS Trusts of social media for patient and public engagement has not yet given rise to widespread use by individual health professionals.

CHAPTER 8

Ethical, Moral and Legal Considerations of Using Social Media in Healthcare Information

Introduction

As with any technology in use in healthcare – and many other settings – there are a number of ethical and moral considerations that need to be observed for the safety, privacy and security of all users: those who create the content and those who consume it. Wolfe et al. (2021) have highlighted some of the issues around ethical considerations of social media in healthcare, including maintaining patient privacy, ensuring any conflicts of interest are proclaimed and exercising due care when using social media to engage patients, educate the public and marketing.

As well as national and international legislation and guidelines, we are all bound – as are our users – by organisational policies and guidelines. It would be a rare hospital Trust or university that would not have guidelines and policies in place around the use of social media in the 2020s, although there are vast variations between organisations.

According to Coburn (2021), librarians are one of the most trusted professions (right after nurses). We can use that reputation in our efforts to ensure that social media in healthcare is used as ethically, morally and responsibly as possible.

Confidentiality, privacy and security

Ensuring the privacy, security and confidentiality of patients or service users – and that of ourselves and colleagues too – should be at the very top of the list of ethical considerations.

As healthcare information professionals, we are similarly bound by both the relevant legislation of our own territories or jurisdictions and by the guidance of our professional membership organisations. CILIP, for example, explicitly states our responsibility to ensure 'confidentiality of information provided by clients or users and the right of all individuals to privacy' in the *Ethical Principles and Code of Professional Practice* (CILIP, 2018). The American Library Association (ALA) is clear on its stance on maintaining privacy (ALA, 2018; ALA, 2021) and the International Federation of Library Associations and Institutions (IFLA) has briefly outlined the history of maintaining the privacy of library patrons in recent years, but expressed concern around the implications of some of the newer technologies affecting us. This particularly applies to artificial intelligence (AI) but also to traditional library activities. This includes data analytics. We are also required to exercise due diligence around third-party product licensing and what vendors are allowed to do with the data collected about users.

As healthcare information professionals, we can ensure that we maintain knowledge of when guidelines are updated – possibly using social media to alert us. We can also help to develop case studies on the responsible use of personal data of our users.

As well as the guidelines from membership organisations, many institutions have developed policies around professionalism that can help physicians and clinicians avoid lapses in professionalism. All registered healthcare professionals are bound by the Code of Conduct of their particular Royal College or membership body, from the British Medical Association (BMA) to the Royal College of Nursing (RCN), the Nursing and Midwifery Council (NMC), the Royal College of Physicians and the Royal College of Psychiatrists.

Many of these bodies issue clear, regularly updated guidance on the use of social media and some have also made example case studies available (HCPC, 2022).

The views of the general public, however, remain relatively poorly understood although what is known is that perceived inappropriate use of social media can damage trust in clinicians (Fatollahi et al., 2020). Some studies have found that one of the major concerns for the public is the use of their data, resulting in reluctance to use social media as a tool for healthcare. For researchers, ensuring the online privacy of research recruits is paramount.

User security and privacy on social media

Issues of security and privacy, as well as preserving confidentiality, are some of the most important ethical considerations healthcare professionals, including healthcare information professionals, need to ensure they take into account when using social media. In recent years, healthcare information is an area that has come under threat from increasingly severe cyberattacks (Devi, 2023; Harish et al., 2023). Social media can also be an unfortunately efficient and effective way of spreading information about such attacks (Shrestha et al., 2020).

Concerns about privacy were shown to be a barrier for healthcare providers wishing to use social media for health purposes, although in general, professionals ranked concerns about privacy lower than patients did (Fisher and Clayton, 2012). Sadly, concerns about privacy on the part of patients often turn out to be valid, even where the original intentions of the healthcare provider have been for the best (Ahmed et al., 2020).

When healthcare providers are able to tap into clearer training around the ethical and responsible use of online communication channels and methods, it's hoped that the risks of this type of potential violation will decrease. Hospital librarians and those working with patient information need to be especially alert to potential breaches of ethics. Breaches of privacy on social media can result in substantial sanctions for healthcare organisations, from reputational damage to hefty fines (Seh et al., 2020).

One way to overcome the potential barrier of privacy is for healthcare information professionals to encourage healthcare professionals to use private messaging or to signpost to channels that are able to ensure high levels of personal privacy and confidentiality. Another is to use an encrypted platform to communicate. WhatsApp is one option; others include Telegram and Signal.

Protecting our own privacy online

How secure or private users want to make their social media activity is, to some extent, a matter of personal choice. Different social media platforms have different privacy settings. Facebook, for example, lets users fine-tune privacy settings to choose exactly who can see their posts. It is also possible to control how easily others can find a profile. X allows users to make tweets private, visible only to approved users and many community websites and forums offer a variety of privacy options.

Whatever options are selected, privacy (and confidentiality) can be difficult to guarantee, even in closed groups or forums. While a good rule is never to share or reveal anything on social media that you wouldn't be happy to see printed in a newspaper, social media is once again something of a double-edged sword here. On the one hand, anyone can express their opinion, but with so many opinions, disagreements can be inevitable. Unfortunately, in recent years an unpleasant and uncivil tone has been all too apparent in some areas of social media, with abuse, harassment and trolling sometimes characterising exchanges of opinion.

Trolling is the term used where a poster on social media seeks to provoke negative responses from others in the online forum. Trolls are distinguished from those who are simply criticising or disagreeing with posters by the fact that they merely want a negative reaction. The increasing use of bots and other automated technologies is another area that can be less than ethical, particularly where the end user does not realise that they are interacting with a machine rather than a human.

It is important that social media users who might encounter opinions or even receive personal messages that hit a nerve maintain their professional detachment and keep matters respectful. The saying 'don't feed the trolls' can be a useful guide in these cases. In many cases the safest approach is not to respond, but if a user deems a response necessary – for example where an untrue statement about the individual user has been made – then as neutral a tone as possible is necessary.

Unfortunately, on occasion, even the organisations we should be able to trust turn out to be less than open about how data is used. Das (2023) reported on an investigation into 20 NHS Trusts which had shared patient data with Facebook. The safest option is to share as little personally identifying data as possible, whatever activity we are involved with on social media, in an effort to protect both ourselves, our service users and their service users.

Patient information and use of social media

Librarians who deal directly with patient information, or work with healthcare professionals who advise those dealing directly with patient information, need to have a strategy in mind for how to respond if patients have questions around health.

The more sensitive the topic, the more important it is to determine how appropriate it is to use social media and the safeguards around that use (Crotty and Mostaghimi, 2014). Another aspect of using social media to interact with patients that is something of an ethical minefield is whether an individual on social media is genuinely who they say they are.

The risk of misinformation, and the potential for litigation, has also led some medical organisations to have a stated policy not to use social media as a channel to issue personalised advice about health conditions. Rather, their social media focuses on how the service can help in general.

Social media platforms are also, unfortunately, notoriously vulnerable to hacking, potentially exposing sensitive patient and personal data. Even those healthcare information professionals who are not directly patient-facing have a responsibility to keep patient data safe and highlight concerns to the appropriate authorities. This is particularly important where it concerns, for example, cyberbullying or potentially misleading information, even in the most supportive of online groups and communities.

Patients need to decide for themselves whether the risks, which can include affecting relationships with clinicians, are worth the benefits (Kanchan and Gaidhane, 2023; Benetoli, Chen and Aslani, 2018). Clinicians also need to weigh up the risks, to themselves and to their patients (van der Boon et al., 2024).

While formal risk assessments are not always a consideration when it comes to the use of social media, it is essential to weigh the potential benefits and risks and ensure that appropriate safeguards are in place. This protects not only patients and service users as much as possible, but helps to maintain professional integrity as healthcare information professionals.

The private–personal contradictions of social media for healthcare professionals

There are also issues around the use of social media where doctors are both doctors facing the public, with a professional reputation to uphold, and private individuals with thoughts and opinions of their own. This came into stark focus during the COVID-19 pandemic.

This contradiction and clash between the public persona of the professional healthcare expert and the human who needed an outlet to cope with the unprecedented difficulties of dealing with a global pandemic was only too apparent in the 'dancing nurses' labelling that surfaced during COVID-19. Lancaster et al. (2022) identified 356 violations of principles from Code of Ethics, the principles of social networking and guidelines for social media in the 52 videos they selected for content analysis. There were also some mainstream media outlets who were quick to denounce the activity (Williams and Duell, 2020). Lancaster et al. (2022) stated concerns around the possible misinterpretation of some of the dance moves and the oversexualisation of the profession. They also expressed concern that such videos could undermine the seriousness of the pandemic and called for nurses to better understand guidelines on workplace and professional use of social media.

Protecting ourselves online

Unfortunately, social media also lends itself all too easily for those who derive pleasure from trolling or even bullying. For those finding messages from someone upsetting or distracting, it is usually possible to block their account, or 'ghost' them in modern terminology. Posts that are harassing, threatening or spam can also be reported to the moderators of the platform. Information on when and how to do this is covered in the help pages of most social media platforms. These include Twitter (X) and Facebook. As it is now illegal to threaten or harass someone online, the police should take any reports seriously.

Social media and the law

There are many benefits to using social media, but the legal consequences of improper use can be serious. Those who fall into this category may run into legal issues like defamation or even contempt of court. Librarians can help clinicians identify the latest guidance from the BMA, GMC or other professional body.

Serious trends on social media: the case of TikTok

Social media can, unfortunately, be extraordinarily insidious and in some cases there have even been cases of deaths among the public resulting from trends on social media. While some are relatively harmless, such as the ice bucket challenge (as long as there are no contraindicated underlying conditions), others are far more harmful.

TikTok often comes in for particular criticism. It has been highlighted, for instance, in cases of what is called 'screen washing', where social media platforms pretend to be far more socially responsible than they are (Koning, van den Eijnden and Vossen, 2024). There are also serious concerns around the handling of personal data by the Chinese-owned platform. At the time of writing, the USA is insistent that TikTok is either sold to a US buyer or banned completely by 2025 (Maheshwari and Holpuch, 2024).

TikTok and the Portrayal of Potentially Harmful Behaviours

One of the major issues identified with information on TikTok is the way that harmful health behaviours are often portrayed. One survey that investigated the metrics around the top 100 videos using the #alcohol hashtag found that 98% of the videos portrayed drinking alcohol in a positive manner. The addition of influencers on Instagram can also be detrimental and librarians can help information users and creators establish whether the information is robustly evidence-based or sponsored by creators or backers who are motivated by finance or reputation.

Other hashtags that bear further scrutiny include #MentalHealth. This hashtag can lead to clips that incorporate 'advice' from self-styled experts (rather than qualified healthcare specialists) on such topics as eating disorders and sex education. Other areas of concern include vaccines and alternative medicine that is unproven, drug regulation and processes and conspiracy theories (Zenone, Ow and Barbic, 2021). Other conditions for which information is found on TikTok include diabetes (author), myopia (Ming et al., 2023), and psoriasis (Aghajani and Aghajani, 2023), with varying levels of reliability.

In addition, TikTok videos are sometimes created as personal stories of surviving difficult life experiences. Although the concept of 'expert by experience' is gaining ground and has been defined, to some extent, by the Care Quality Commission (CQC, 2023) and those who share their stories are regarded as courageous, it can be difficult to ensure that the content does not reach those who are not necessarily prepared to view it. There can also be cases of hate speech including racism or sexism or even xenophobia. Healthcare information professionals may find themselves in a position where they need to guide users or at least help them to understand the need for careful assessment of anything they see or read on screen.

Certain groups, for example adolescents, have been shown to be particularly vulnerable to misinformation on the platform as well as to enticements to take part in 'challenges' that are potentially extremely dangerous.

The Tide Pod Challenge

The Tide Pod Challenge was a short-lived but incredibly dangerous internet trend that emerged in late 2017. It involved a small number of people, primarily teenagers, recording themselves biting into Tide laundry detergent pods and posting the videos online. The pods contain highly concentrated toxic detergent which can be extremely harmful if ingested and in fact at least nine people have died in the USA from ingesting the pods (Meth, 2019). The deaths do not appear to have been a direct result of the 'challenge': two of the deaths were small children and the other seven were elderly individuals with dementia (Meth, 2019). The challenge was, however, a shocking example of how quickly harmful trends can spread online and the potential consequences of such behaviour.

While the platform has strict guidelines against dangerous content, it is sobering to realise that the challenge managed to gain some traction before it was widely condemned and removed. It's important to note that TikTok has since implemented stricter measures to prevent such harmful trends from spreading.

The Benadryl Challenge

The Benadryl Challenge was another highly dangerous trend that involved people, primarily teenagers, consuming excessive amounts of the over-the-counter antihistamine, diphenhydramine (commonly sold as Benadryl), to induce hallucinations. This incredibly risky challenge resulted in severe health consequences, including hospitalisation and even death (Psychiatrist.com, 2023).

Like the Tide Pod Challenge, this dangerous trend spread rapidly among young people. It stands as yet another stark reminder of the potential dangers of social media and the importance of critical thinking. For those in healthcare settings, the duty of care towards users is another factor to consider when using social media. Both the Tide Pod and the Benadryl challenges can be used as clips to illustrate patient education. Searching for evidence and resources is no longer, and has not been for a long time, only about finding papers from academic journals.

These uses of social media have highlighted the likely need in the near future for stricter regulations and restrictions around content as well as monitoring usage. Librarians have a delicate balance to strike here. On the one hand, many librarians are not in favour of censorship. However, most if not all librarians, particularly in healthcare, have a strong sense of responsibility towards their users as well as an understanding of the importance of keeping them safe.

When it comes to mobile media, the ethics are even more complex. There are ethical considerations around the use of mobile imaging and location tracking, for example, even though most of us have our location active on our mobile phones without a second thought.

While the role of a librarian would not be to explicitly tell users what to post on social media, they can offer signposting towards general advice on netiquette, as it was once called. This term encompasses a range of acceptable behaviour online, from courtesy to remembering that, unless your camera is switched on, those you're interacting with cannot see your reactions. It is interesting to note that new releases of Microsoft Teams and others have increased their range of emoticons and reactions in an effort to combat this. Librarians can also consider incorporating information about appropriate use of social media into health literacy instruction sessions along with the responsible use of social media in healthcare patient information.

Social media and medication

Liang and Mackey (2012) are amongst those who have touched on the role of social media with regards to prescription medication. While Sarker et al.

(2016) identified the potential of mining social media for information about potential prescription medication abuse, Willis et al. (2023) have identified the possibility of recruiting 'patient influencers' to communicate 'health literacy' via social media.

As is the case with so many other aspects of social media in healthcare information, however, the use of influence has the potential to be both beneficial and detrimental. At the time of writing, celebrity influencers are endorsing the use of the Type 2 diabetes medication Ozempic as a weight loss drug (Carboni et al., 2024). Those praising the drug on social media appear to be either heedless or indifferent to the potential effects of hoarding on Type 2 diabetics or those with obesity who may need that drug for their condition.

The shortage situation is compounded by recent research suggesting that the US Food and Drug Administration (FDA)-approved anti-obesity medication Wegovy in particular may also have beneficial effects on other conditions, including dementia (Radcliffe Department of Medicine, 2024). In many cases, such research is picked up by social media and condensed into a microblog or post which may or may not be accurate. The skills of librarians in healthcare information are invaluable in helping to establish the reliability of such claims – and the original research – as well as recommending evidence-based sources to their users.

Virtual worlds

Launched in 2003, Linden Labs' Second Life interactive 'virtual world' was hailed as a huge step forward. Using avatars, participants could collaborate, shop and generally interact with each other in 'real time'.

The platform was originally devised as a kind of online exploration lab for the company's work on haptics, a particular kind of technology that allows the user to experience tactile sensations via the application of force, vibrations, or motions. The platform's potential for health-related activities and education has been explored, with applications in medical training, patient–doctor interactions and anatomy visualisation (Schwaab et al., 2011). However, research suggests that Second Life offered little unique value compared to other online health resources (Suomi, Mäntymäki and Söderlund, 2014).

While Second Life's popularity has waned, its concept and design has influenced recent developments in virtual reality. This includes Meta's Metaverse initiative (Gent, 2021). The experience of Second Life provides valuable lessons for future virtual world endeavours, particularly in areas of user engagement, content reliability and practical applications.

Other serious situations on social media have arisen in recent virtual worlds, with the Metaverse in particular cited in some very unpleasant situations, including cases of virtual assault (Marr, 2024). The issues around AI and virtual reality are likely to be increasingly problematic as the technology matures, especially where combined with social media and personalisation.

While science bounds ahead – and internet technology and developments are part of that scientific landscape – the laws that are there to protect us often lag behind. They are reactive rather than predictive. The issue of whether scientists in particular should move forward with their developments just because they can has been explored in fiction for centuries, as Dr Victor Frankenstein could attest (Shelley, 1818).

Other ethical considerations

Ethical considerations around the use of information are far from new or unique to social media. Intellectual property, copyright, the potential for negligence and issues around ensuring the privacy of individuals have all been areas of concern for many decades.

In a world where most countries can access information on the internet with relative ease, there are also cross-border differences to consider. What is acceptable in relatively open societies like the UK, Europe or the USA, for instance, may be censored – at best – in some other parts of the world, as the COVID-19 experience of China bears out. Ensuring familiarity with the codes outlined by the professional information management organisations in individual countries can help to demonstrate awareness, although should situations escalate to requiring legal input, it is also wise to remember that guidance is not law.

Healthcare information professionals can help to both protect themselves and inform their users about the pitfalls by ensuring that they are as up-to-date as possible with appropriate legislation around areas like data protection, privacy, copyright and plagiarism, defamation, breach of duty of care and accessibility.

While the need for highly specialised technical skills is less of an issue with social media, one area that is likely to grow in importance is an understanding of the ethical, moral and social implications of information that has not been peer-reviewed and that is largely user-generated. The skills required to assess information objectively and rationally are not as widespread as might be hoped, as some aspects of the COVID-19 pandemic showed.

There are also environmental issues to consider around the use of social media, particularly as it starts to combine with AI. In a world where resources are increasingly scarce and climate change now undeniable, social media, smartphones and AI are all extremely resource-hungry. This applies both to the minerals that make them possible in the first place and the server power they demand.

Social media: positive moral aspects

Although this chapter has largely focused on the challenging aspects of the morality and ethics of using social media, it also has the potential to be a force for good. It can, for example, level the playing field when it comes to providing information for traditionally marginalised groups. This may include those in the LGBTQIA+ community, those who are neurodiverse and those with a disability.

Social media in its most basic forms can also be used to reach those in resource-poor parts of the world or even our own homelands. Increasingly, it is possible to translate social media posts into languages other than English and from English into those other languages. While the last few years have hardly given much cause for optimism, it is possible, in time, that a more balanced distribution of social media could allow us to move away from our current developed-world narrative, dominated by the USA. It may even afford us a more equitable view of global issues – and even potential solutions.

The role of the librarian

Librarians can also help to support their users by maintaining up-to-date knowledge of general legislation and guidance, as well as working with their organisations to develop good-practice guidelines on the use of social media. Showcasing the positive and judicious use of social media in case studies and emphasising the collated benefits for patients can also help.

CHAPTER 9

The Future of Social Media in Healthcare Information

Introduction

While there is no foolproof way of predicting the future, we can find hints about probable future trajectories by both looking at past developments and by understanding likely trends. They can act as an early warning, as it were, for skills that healthcare information professionals may need to acquire or to help their colleagues to acquire.

Social media is affected by technological advancements and societal shifts, as well as user preferences. As artificial intelligence (AI) becomes more integrated with social media, it's likely that content will become more tailored and feeds far more personalised. Augmented reality filters like those used in the Pokémon Go craze of 2016 may also be of use in both encouraging increased physical activity (Piqueras-Sola et al., 2024; Baronowski and Lyons, 2020) and medical and healthcare education applications (Wan, 2017). Not only that, but the filters and effects will become more sophisticated. There may also be a move towards more decentralised social networks, as users gain more control over their data. This may allay some of the current fears around privacy and security of personal data.

The bulk of this book has been concerned with where we are now and to some extent how we got here with regard to social media. It's therefore timely to consider where we've been; and where we might go next.

User education

While promotion of a library and its offer has always been a major focus for social media pages for both academic and public libraries, there are no rules around combining these with content that also has an element of learning or education. Some platforms, such as Facebook, lend themselves particularly well to asynchronous learning and discussions and many social media platforms offer polling features to collect opinions, feedback and questions from users. For Wenger (1998), sharing, discussing and learning are the ways that students and librarians show their involvement or engagement with their online community of practice.

When it comes to education, podcasts and video tutorials offer healthcare librarians the chance to increase the accessibility of complex health information, making it accessible to a wider audience. The use of hashtags and user-generated 'folksonomies' also allow health librarians to curate and disseminate healthcare information using 'real-world' vocabulary. Healthcare librarians have been able to effectively leverage social media to connect with communities. Patient and public engagement is likely to continue to become more important, with healthcare information professionals sharing updates on research, including the promotion of research conducted by students and faculty, along with information about library resources and details of practice guidelines which are firmly based in evidence. As databases, journals and other resources evolve and merge, healthcare information professionals will also be able to draw the attention of users and potentially increase and target information.

Demonstrating impact

It is likely that the necessity to demonstrate the impact of libraries will continue and social media use will not be exempt from this. There are, however, queries around how we demonstrate impact and whether simply assessing engagement levels will be sufficient – whatever form those levels may take. Gerlitz and Helmond (2013) describe 'social media engagement' in terms of clicks, where users 'like' or 'heart' posts.

The Internet of Things

The Internet of Things is another development that potentially makes use of social media for its infrastructure and function. While 5G remains an elusive dream in much of the UK, once it is more widespread there are options for improved communication and a more robust Internet of Things network.

Since, at the time of writing, there are still areas of the UK that have no 4G or very limited coverage (Baker and Hutton, 2022) and barely scrape a 3G signal, it seems somewhat premature to be thinking about 6G networks, but apparently they are on the horizon. If and when they materialise, they may offer still more improved potential for communication, including social-media adjacent developments like artificial intelligence and holographic messaging (Calvanese Strinati et al., 2019). It's also likely that the current boundaries between social media, mobile health or mHealth, wearables, games and the big data that can include our health information will blur.

While mobile technology and the fact that the iPad and other tablets have brought some benefits such as alternative communication and augmented reality, they have also brought challenges such as digital exclusion. For those areas that are left behind, including many rural locations, the digital divide is likely to increase. Fitbits and blood glucose monitors, for instance, often use apps linked to location or biometrics to alert their users to changes in readings. Collated data from several sources may provide invaluable insights from an epidemiological perspective; the challenge is how to analyse this data without compromising the privacy of individuals.

The skills which we will need, as information professionals in a healthcare setting, are both technical and transferable, traditional and cutting-edge. We will need to understand coding, for example and the implications of metadata; we will also need to demonstrate flexibility and discrimination in what we choose to incorporate into our service. As is the case with many scientific developments, just because something exists or suddenly appears does not mean that we have to implement them straight away – or indeed at all.

As we move into the next age of the internet, where AI and social media are likely to mesh, where mHealth becomes a feasible option for clinicians to monitor the health of their patients remotely, the role of the librarian, information scientist or healthcare information professional will evolve further. Librarians may also find themselves called upon to assist users with some basic operation of devices, for example blood pressure monitors. Public libraries in England that have taken part in pilot schemes include Cornwall, Somerset and Hampshire as part of the then UK government's 'Health on the High Street' initiative, often working in conjunction with co-located health professionals (DCMS, 2022).

Infodemiology

What Eysenbach called 'infodemiology' (2009) is also likely to become increasingly important. Infodemiology, which can be defined as 'the science of distribution and determinants of information in an electronic medium . . . with the ultimate aim to inform public health and . . . policy' is a particularly promising approach, due to its capacity for collecting and analysing 'real-time' data. Eysenbach highlighted examples including data from internet search engines that would allow the prediction of outbreaks of disease; identifying what we would now term the 'health information gap' or 'health inequality' in terms of accessing information; and monitoring the success of health campaigns.

Future healthcare information professionals are well placed to use their skills and expertise to help healthcare professionals navigate the ever-changing landscape of technology, as well as share their knowledge with both service users and colleagues. By following 'thought leaders' on social media, we can also help to make efficient use of what is often one of the most precious and rare commodities – time.

Web 2.0 to Web 3.0: an inevitable transition?

The Web 2.0 technology that underpins social media has revolutionised some of the roles health librarians traditionally assume, allowing new and innovative ways of engaging with users. As well as sharing health information, answering questions and building relationships with the user community, health sciences librarians can build blogs and wikis, online forums and discussion groups.

According to Tattersall, Beecroft and Cantrell (2011), it was the transition of the original internet to Web 2.0 that allowed us to communicate, research, work, promote ourselves and our interests and, above all, collaborate. If Web 1.0 was the original internet and we are currently approaching the end of Web 2.0, what is 'Web 3.0' likely to look like?

The logical progression from Web 2.0 might be thought to be Web 3.0, sometimes referred to as the Semantic Web (Gan et al., 2023; Nasar, 2023; Anwar, 2022). Web 3.0 is likely to build on the social networking aspects of Web 2.0, extending its reach to incorporate artificial intelligence (AI) and possibly transaction systems like blockchain. Web 3.0 technologies take the collaborative and interactive aspects of Web 2.0 one step further. These developments include cloud computing, augmented reality and big data. Learners who have been traditionally passive will become active participants (Hussain, 2012). Challenges, however, will remain around security and privacy risks, the accessibility of the web, how ready users are to navigate Web 3.0 and the potential broadening of digital inequalities.

It is also pertinent to consider the current dominance of certain social media channels or sites. Facebook continues to dominate, but others, notably X, are showing signs of decay that cannot be ignored. Although it is still used extensively, the nature of the network has changed dramatically since its purchase by Elon Musk, becoming more overtly commercial and political. At present there is no obvious successor. Although sites such as Threads, Jack Dorsey's Bluesky and Mastodon are potential competitors, no single network at the time of writing has managed to quite achieve the reach of X in the days when it was Twitter and not just what Potter (2023) has described as a 'wasteland'.

In Web 3.0, discoverability is the aim, sometimes referred to as findability. With the sheer volume of academic literature alone now in the public domain, it is likely that Web 3.0, combined with AI, will allow us to develop and implement more effective, more efficient ways of searching, collating and disseminating. We do, however, need to guard against the tendencies of some AI to hallucinate, or simply make it all up.

Health Librarian 3.0: future-proofing the profession

What was noticeable in the compilation of this book is that the issues around the use of social media in healthcare information are not limited only to the UK, or North America, Australasia, the Middle or Far East, or the Global South: they're universal. The internet changes at an incredible pace. Tattersall (2011) identified the relentless and inevitable march towards both a 'mobile and Semantic Web', taking us ever deeper into the cloud. Tattersall also compares the web to a new land in this paper, highlighting how, as in a colony, many of the early sites (or settlements) simply collapsed and vanished. As we move forward, what skills are librarians likely to need?

The role of medical library services is a crucial one for patient care. Our role as healthcare information professionals is to ensure that we facilitate access to the most up-to-date clinical guidelines, research and resources (Lacey Bryant et al., 2022) – whatever form that may take.

Healthcare information professionals are likely to find themselves having to find ways to cope with end-to-end encryption, whether that is assisting users or advocating to organisational IT departments for fewer barriers for certain classes of information.

Crowdsourcing data may be a further development for healthcare information providers, allowing them to promote health literacy and subsequently improve patient care. The use of social media for quick-reference questions is another potential cost-effective approach, although carrying out evaluation of the use of social media and its impact is likely to remain a challenge beyond simple usage statistics.

Understanding how social media users search the various platforms and which demographics are most likely to be drawn to particular platforms can also be invaluable when it comes to planning healthcare library use.

While many users will head straight for the platform-specific search bars on a platform, some platforms also include internal search functions that can allow users to seek specific keywords, accounts, or hashtags, as well as date, location, or even type or length of content. The use of niche hashtags can result in more targeted information and results – helping save users time and improving the user experience. Health sciences librarians can also help social media platform users identify the credentials of influencers, the motives behind user-generated content and the levels of reliability of social media content.

Big data

More integration of data sources to give a 'big data' overview is another field that is likely to require information management skills and input from healthcare information professionals.

By its very nature, big data is complex and grows exponentially over time. For an accurate picture, many different sources need to be considered, as outlined by Pastorino et al. (2019). Healthcare information professionals are particularly well placed to support these developments, thereby contributing to the future healthcare needs of society, although it is likely that new skills will need to be acquired, including coding, statistical analysis and new methods of interpretation and presentation. Healthcare librarians have the chance to be instrumental in providing data-driven insights to healthcare providers, whether these take the form of sentiment analysis, epidemic tracking, or trend analysis. Ensuring that researchers are aware of potential algorithmic bias can help combat the unintentional perpetuating of health disparities, while ensuring that both accountability and informed consent are taken into account can potentially avoid legislative and ethical challenges.

It's probable that information on social media will continue to be predominantly visual in nature, with short-form video platforms like TikTok setting the trend, at least in the short term. Along with that, platform-specific features such as duets, stitches and live reactions will increase in popularity. Another potential development lies in more specialised platforms and a reversion to content recommended by followers or the community rather than algorithms.

The role of artificial intelligence (AI)

Although AI is increasingly significant and interwoven with social media, it has not (yet) replaced it and it isn't always obvious when AI is being used. It can, for instance, underlie the recommendations of content based on user preferences, including videos or posts. Increasingly, AI is the technology that underpins chatbots and customer service. Although ChatGPT is one of the best known large-language models or LLMs, its use within medical libraries remains largely theoretical at present, as Lund, Khan and Yuvaraj (2024) have identified. There is still a great need for human input, particularly in the training of large-language models: AI has to be 'taught' how to write (or, more accurately, generate predictive content), how to 'see' and how to interpret the data it sees.

There may be more success for the use of AI in image and video analysis, with notable recent projects including fracture detection on radiographs (Suen, Zhang and Kutaiba, 2024); mammograms (Xavier et al., 2024); and MRI in rheumatology (Adams et al., 2024) amongst others. Healthcare librarians can help support service users with literature searches and 'lessons learned' that can feed into quality improvement projects and more.

AI may also be able to identify and prevent the creation of fake accounts and simultaneously create avatars or virtual characters. A further possible application for AI which may be of use in healthcare information is its ability to break down language barriers for global communication. As Kamadjeu (2019), amongst others, has identified, the majority of scientific research is produced in English, but in recent years some authors have also chosen to write in languages other than English (Solli and Ødemark, 2019).

Although Google Translate is one option and nothing compares with human translated text, AI can offer a draft translation that can serve as a rough guide to the contents of a document, helping to break down language barriers for global communication. Some types of AI can also help create a more inclusive social media experience for people with disabilities, for example text-to-voice or natural language to British Sign Language (or American Sign Language or other variants).

At present, AI-powered and assisted search is in its early days but is likely to revolutionise the way in which search results are organised and disseminated in future. As well as improved search algorithms which may or may not deliver more relevant and accurate health information based on user queries, AI may also be able to identify and flag health content that is false or misleading.

As AI evolves, mutates, changes and morphs, it may even be able to transform into a virtual health assistant. In some cases, it may have the capacity to offer personalised support and guidance for those managing chronic conditions, particularly where the AI is combined with wearable sensors (Shajari et al., 2023).

AI may also be able to facilitate connections between patients with the same or similar conditions, fostering not only support but sharing of information to help build a forum or community.

The human connection

What has become apparent since COVID-19, however, is that what healthcare information professionals can provide which AI cannot is human connection, interaction and human-filtered content creation. In some ways, this is the internet coming full circle. In the early days, Yahoo and other online directories had substantial human input.

While the integration of AI into some aspects of social media is already well under way, deeper future integration might include predictive content, AI-generated content including images, videos and text and real-time content moderation. AI, if correctly programmed and configured, may be able to identify and remove harmful content including misinformation and hate speech 'on the fly'. Some of the inappropriate content that can cause distress to unwary users may therefore be filtered out before it even reaches them.

Librarians can also help their cause by choosing the right platforms, ones which align with the target audience and goals and incorporate images, infographics, video and sound clips to get a message across. Tracking analytics by monitoring performance and engagement levels and adjusting strategies accordingly is another invaluable tool.

Conclusion

In the 50-plus years since the concept became a reality, the internet has changed the world we live in beyond recognition and continues to do so. It was designed for co-operation and instantaneous information dissemination, at a time when idealism was far higher and cynicism far lower than today.

In the same time frame, healthcare has also made immense strides forward. Clinicians and scientists have worked out how to transplant organs to extend life, how to cure some forms of cancer and how to diagnose some health conditions in the very earliest stages at which they pose a potential threat to the carrier.

When a global pandemic threatened the world – and tragically, killed and incapacitated far too many – the power of social media was apparent as an information force for both the benefit and detriment of humanity. Scientists were able to track the disease in 'real time', combining this with behavioural science insights into behavioural psychology that, in some cases, encouraged responsible actions to help limit the spread. Social media offered a way to communicate evidence-based news instantaneously. It was both a balm to assuage fears and a vessel for misinformation and conspiracy theories.

During the pandemic, education, working life and healthcare were transformed as online meetings software like Zoom and Microsoft Teams became accessible to the many, not just the fortunate few in highly academic settings. Universities and other seats of learning saw the potential of this new mode of working and used the channels to deliver lectures, discussions and even webinars during lockdowns. GPs and others were able to offer remote consultations – teleconsults, effectively. In a world where more than one generation had never known anything but an always-connected, always-on environment it can hardly be surprising that their first choice of media channel for information about COVID-19 was often social media.

Predicting the future remains an imprecise art, but what is possible is to look at current developments in a field and make educated guesses about the likely trajectory. With that in mind, these are just some of the likely developments that may lie ahead with the next iteration of social media:

- AI, including LLMs and AR
- combating misinformation
- education
- ensuring organisations are aware of ethical frameworks and legislations by increasing involvement with policy making
- health literacy
- information searching
- information seeking
- information synthesis
- involvement with policies
- partnerships and collaboration – as the original creators of ARPANET intended
- research.

And as AI begins to take shape as what is almost certainly the next big technology that will affect us all, clinicians have begun to use it in diagnoses and interventions (Alowais et al., 2023) along with other techniques like machine learning (Connor et al., 2021).

For librarians, health information professionals, information officers, information scientists and all the other myriad names that encompass those who work in the information sector, there are several implications for our practice as we learn to navigate a world that marries AI and social media.

Overcoming barriers

There are still far too many barriers to overcome, particularly in low- to medium-income countries, the Global South and even pockets of the G7 nations, including the UK. As always it's probable that progress will be erratic and it's possible that it will take several turns sideways and even regress. What is fairly certain is that one day we are likely to look around and wonder what happened to what we now know as social media, along with dot.com millionaires, Friendster and Friends Reunited. It's also likely that the technology itself will change. At present, the concept of data projected into the ether is still (mostly) a high-end concept, but as haptic gloves become more powerful, the idea of 'web anywhere' is likely to become a literal reality.

The new paradigm may be called Web 4.0 or AIweb or Social AI, although whatever it ends up being called it probably won't be until at least a decade from now that we're able to look back and begin to understand the longitudinal impact. The Semantic Web is all about links – literally, the web of information. Health librarians are also likely to be well placed to test the new semantic technologies and assess methods of integrating them into what can be described as our legacy systems.

Those of us who may work in environments where much new technology is viewed with suspicion or apprehension will need to draw on all our resourcefulness, persistence and advocacy skills to encourage IT departments and board members to see the advantages of social media, just as we needed to when Web 2.0 technologies were in their infancy. We also need to guard against the use of a single source as justification for arguments and decisions.

Once again, we will need to take every opportunity to reposition ourselves as expert information facilitators and educators and as arbiters and interpreters of accurate, evidence-based information.

Glossary of Social Media Terms

Algorithm: Each social media platform has an underlying list of rules that are used to determine what content users see. Algorithms have become controversial in recent years, owing to manipulation behind the scenes in election campaigns and where promotion of content has been paid for or otherwise manipulated.

ALIA: Australian Library and Information Association.

Analytics: Term applied to data collected and analysed to understand user behaviour and performance on a platform.

Augmented reality: This is a live direct – or indirect – view of a real-world physical environment where virtual, computer-generated imagery is used to augment various elements. The technology, which usually requires a virtual reality headset, glasses or other camera- and sensor-enabled device, enhances the user's current perception of reality. Example: Pokémon Go, summer 2016.

Avatar: In computing, gaming, or information applications, an icon or figure representing a specific individual in a video game or internet forum.

Blackboard: A virtual learning environment used in many universities and other academic organisations around the world. It allows educators to make content available to learners and manage classes online. Increasingly elements such as wikis, blogs, RSS and virtual reality learning spaces are features of the system.

Blog: Short for 'weblog'; blogs are one of the longest-established of the Web 2.0 technologies. A blog is usually an online journal, either literally an online diary or an account of activity in an organisation. Most blogs are informal in tone. The majority are personal and/or non-commercial, although some companies and academic journals have launched their own blogs, for example *The New England Journal of Medicine* and the *BMJ* Group.

Blogosphere: The 'world of' blogs along with their connections.

Blogpost or blog post: An entry in a blog.

CDC: Centers for Disease Control and Prevention. In the USA this organisation is the leading service that protects the health of the public. It is data-driven and science-based and works to protect the USA from internal and external threats relating to security, safety and health.

CILIP: The Chartered Institute of Library and Information Professionals. This is the professional body for information professionals formed in 2002 by the amalgamation of the Library Association and the Institute of Information Scientists in 2002.

CME: Continuing medical education.

Comment: Adding a text-based response to a post.

CPD: Continuing professional development.

Crowdsourcing: The practice of enlisting the services of a large number of people to obtain information or input into a task or project, either paid or unpaid, typically via the internet.

Cyberspace: The virtual computer world, typically involving a large computer network made up of subnetworks of computers around the world. The TCP/IP protocol is used to assist with data exchange and communication: the environment is interactive, allowing users to share information as well as play games, swap ideas, interact with others and exchange information. Science fiction author William Gibson coined the phrase in his 1984 novel *Neuromancer*. Over the years the term has come to be used for a wide range of virtual interfaces.

DM: Direct Message; a message sent via a platform's inbuilt e-mail or messaging system. It makes the privacy of the content far more likely.

Duet: Creating a video alongside another user's video on TikTok.

EAHIL: European Association of Health Information and Libraries. This European organisation aims to unite and motivate librarians and information officers. The purpose is to exchange best practice and knowledge.

Engagement: Interactions with content. This may take the form of likes, comments, shares and clicks.

Explore: A Snapchat section featuring popular posts and content.

Facebook: A social networking platform where users can connect with friends and family, and share photos and videos. They can also interact with businesses and public figures. Rebranded as Meta Platforms, Inc. on 28 October, 2021 although the Facebook branding has been retained.

FDA: Food and Drug Administration: The FDA regulates the safety of food, drugs, medical devices, cosmetics, tobacco products and radiation-emitting products. For example, the FDA approves all medical devices before they can be sold to consumers.

Folksonomy: A system of classification derived from collaboratively assigning tags to categorise content on a website. Also sometimes referred to as social tagging.

Followers: Users who make the choice to subscribe to another user's content, which usually means they will be alerted to stories and updates.

For You Page (FYP): A personalised feed of recommended videos on TikTok.

Friend: A connection on Facebook.

Friend of a Friend (FOAF): An ontology language used to create machine-readable pages of metadata that describes people, as well as the links between them and the things they create and do.

GIS: Geographic Information Systems. In medicine, they may be used to track the location of an ambulance, for example.

Group: A space for people with shared interests to connect on Facebook.

Handle: A username on a social media platform (e.g. @username such as @bbc). It's often possible to send a direct message by, for instance, tweeting @username.

Haptics: Haptic technology uses an operator's sense of touch to allow interaction via computer technology with virtual and remote objects. In medicine, haptic feedback is a method that allows learning by simulation.

Hashtag: Frequently used by Twitter (X) users to make it easier to categorise tweets and now used on many social media platforms. The term describes a keyword or phrase preceded by a # symbol which allows the text to be used as a tag and a search term.

Hi5: A social networking site founded by Ramu Yalamanchi in 2003, one of the 40 most visited websites in the world at its zenith, until its popularity declined. It became a social gaming site in 2010 and is now similar to Tinder; users are able to create profiles and play social games online.

Influencer: An individual with a significant following who is able to 'influence' the opinions and behaviours of others. Many influencers are celebrities who are paid or otherwise sponsored by brands to 'like' particular products or make particular claims.

Instagram: A photo and video-sharing platform using mobile technology. Although it is possible to prepare Instagram stories via traditional apps it is easiest to use smartphones.

Internet of Things: The IoT, as it is sometimes called, refers to a network of physical devices embedded with software and network connectivity, as well as sensors, that allow them to both collect and share data. These devices can include smart lightbulbs, plugs and thermostats, and wearables like Fitbits and other smartwatches.

Like: A positive reaction to a post particularly on Facebook, Instagram or X, sometimes showing as a thumbs-up.

Metadata: Data about data. This may be, for example, details of a social media post's author, content, links or other information to help identify the unique characteristics of the post.

Microblog: A very short blog entry. Microblog entries can consist of short fragments of sentences, images or embedded video.

Netvibes: A personalised, widget-based web publishing platform that uses a dashboard to provide integrated access to a set of digital resources.

NHS, National Health Service: The NHS is the UK's national publicly funded healthcare service. It was founded in 1948. The term refers specifically to the service operating in England; NHS Scotland, NHS Wales and, in Northern Ireland, the Health and Social Care (HSC) are used in their respective parts of the UK

NHS Acute Trust: An Acute Trust is the formally constituted body that manages a hospital in the NHS. Acute Trusts usually have an accident and emergency department attached. The term may also be used to refer to the hospital in question.

NHS Digital: The national information and technology partner of NHS England.

NHS England: Organisation that oversees the provision of public healthcare in England.

NHS Foundation Trust: A Foundation Trust is an independent legal entity that manages an NHS hospital that provides NHS care to NHS patients. As a self-governing organisation it has more autonomy over its decisions than some other types of Trust.

NHS Partnership Trust: An NHS Trust that is responsible, often in collaboration with social services departments in local government authorities, for delivering mental health services.

NHS Teaching Trust: An NHS teaching hospital or Trust is affiliated with a medical school. It provides medical education to students, interns, residents, as well as postgraduates in some cases.

NHS Trust: A formally constituted NHS body responsible for managing an acute, primary care or mental health service.

Ontology: A description of characteristics of data elements and the relationships among them in a particular domain. Ontologies describe many more relationships between terms than is the case with thesauri, as well as multiple kinds of relationships among elements, while taxonomies tend to reveal hierarchical relationships only.

Page: A profile for businesses, organisations, or public figures on Facebook.

Playlist: A collection of videos, especially on TikTok or YouTube.

Podcast: A series of digital multimedia files delivered over the internet for playback on a computer or mobile device. Formerly known as a webcast, the name podcast reflects the one-time popularity of Apple's iPod device for this purpose.

Reel: Short-form video content on platforms like Instagram, Snapchat and TikTok.

Retweet: Sharing someone else's tweet on Twitter (X).

RSS: Really Simple Syndication (also known as Rich Site Summary). An automated web-based feed for distributing news, journal tables of contents and other updated information.

SDI: Selective Dissemination of Information: A current awareness service, typically provided by a library, that provides clients with information on the latest publications in their specified area of interest.

Second Life: A free, three-dimensional virtual world in which users, represented by avatars, are able to socialise, connect and create and trade virtual property or services. Owned by Linden Labs and 21 years old in 2024.

Semantic Web: A term coined by the W3C and Sir Tim Berners-Lee to describe a new stage in the evolution of the web. Data descriptions make it possible to gather information from disparate sources, internal and external to an organisation, as well as to browse, federate and query the information.

Semantics: From the Greek to give signs, meaning, or make significant. Semantics refers to aspects of meaning as expressed in language or other systems of signs.

Share: Distribute content to other users.

Shorts: Short-form video content, especially on TikTok or YouTube.

Stitch: Using a part of another user's video on your own on TikTok.

Story: A short-lived, disappearing post on platforms like Instagram (within 24 hours) and Snapchat.

Subscribe: Social media users subscribe to a social media channel for updates, particularly on TikTok. The equivalent for Facebook, X and other social media platforms is 'Follow'.

TikTok: A short-form video-sharing platform which has grown rapidly since its launch. In September 2024 it had over 1 billion monthly global users.

Trend: A popular topic on Twitter (X).

Tweet: A post on Twitter (X); originally limited to 140 characters and often sent from a mobile (cell) phone. In 2017 the limit was doubled to 280 characters.

Twitter: Former name of X. The website-based platform offers a worldwide social networking and microblogging service. Users can send messages ('tweets') via mobile (cell) phone or the internet.

Twitterverse: The cyberspace universe occupied by Twitter (X) and its users.

Video: Short, creative videos with music, effects and filters, especially on TikTok.

Virtual reality: An artificial but life-like environment created by computers and programmers.

Web 3.0: A contested term used by some to describe the third generation of the web from 2011 to 2020.

WHO: World Health Organization. Established in 1948, the WHO is the directing and co-ordinating authority for health within the United Nations system.

Widget: A small portable code element embedded in a web page that allows the user to customise or interact with a specific feature of the interface.

Wiki: A collaborative website that allows a group of users to share in creating, editing and commenting on content. The word is thought to derive from the Hawaiian word for 'quick' but is also sometimes said to be an acronym for 'what I know is'.

Wikipedia: The largest wiki in the world.

World Wide Web Consortium (W3C): Develops 'interoperable technologies (specifications, standards, software and tools)' for enhancing the web, including HTML, DHTML, XML and many others. See W3C's Semantic Web Health Care and Life Sciences (HCLS) Interest Group, http://esw.w3.org/HCLSIG.

WYSIWYG (What You See Is What You Get): The term describes a computer–user interface in which what appears on the screen is broadly the same as the final output. It is commonly applied to word processing and desktop publishing applications.

YouTube: A website that allows users to upload, share, view and comment on videos. It is used extensively by creatives to disseminate user-generated content and many institutions increasingly set up channels to distribute their own videos.

References and Bibliography

Aced, C. (2013) *Web 2.0: The Origin of the Word that has Changed the Way We Understand Public Relations,* International PR 2013 Conference: Images of Public Relations, www.researchgate.net/publication/266672416_Web_20_the_origin_of_the_word_that_has_changed_the_way_we_understand_public_relations.

Adams, L. C., Bressem, K. K., Ziegeler, K., Vahldiek, J. L. and Poddubnyy, D. (2024) Artificial Intelligence to Analyze Magnetic Resonance Imaging in Rheumatology, *Joint Bone Spine,* **91** (3), 105651, https://doi.org/10.1016/j.jbspin.2023.105651.

Adebesin, F., Smuts, H., Mawela, T., Maramba, G. and Hattingh, M. (2023) The Role of Social Media in Health Misinformation and Disinformation during the COVID-19 Pandemic: Bibliometric Analysis, *JMIR Infodemiology,* **3**, e48620, https://doi.org/10.2196/48620.

Afanasyev, D. O., Fedorova, E. and Ledyaeva, S. (2021) Strength of Words: Donald Trump's Tweets, Sanctions and Russia's Ruble, *Journal of Economic Behavior & Organization,* **184** (3), 253–77, https://doi.org/10.1016/j.jebo.2021.02.002.

Aghajani, M. J. and Aghajani, R. (2023) TikTok and #psoriasis: a Cross-Sectional Study of Content Quality, *Australasian Journal of Dermatology,* **64** (4), e369–e371, https://doi.org/10.1111/ajd.14149.

Ahmed, W., Jagsi, R., Gutheil, T. G. and Katz, M. S. (2020) Public Disclosure on Social Media of Identifiable Patient Information by Health Professionals: Content Analysis of Twitter Data, *Journal of Medical Internet Research,* **22** (9), e19746, https://doi.org/10.2196/19746.

Aichner, T. and Jacob, F. (2015) Measuring the Degree of Corporate Social Media Use, *International Journal of Market Research,* **57** (2), 257–76, https://doi.org/10.2501/IJMR-2015-018.

Aichner, T., Grünfelder, M., Maurer, O. and Jegeni, D. (2021) Twenty-Five Years of Social Media: a Review of Social Media Applications and Definitions from 1994 to 2019, *Cyberpsychology, Behavior, and Social Networking,* **24** (4), 215–22, https://doi.org/10.1089/cyber.2020.0134.

Akers, K. G. (2019) Report from the Medical Library Association's InSight Initiative Summit 2: Meeting the Evolving Information Needs of Library Stakeholders, *Journal of the Medical Library Association,* **107** (2), 137–50, https://doi.org/10.5195/jmla.2019.669.

ALA (American Library Association) (2018) *ALA Privacy Policy,* American Library Association, https://www.ala.org/privacypolicy.

ALA (American Library Association) (2021) Code of Ethics of the American Library Association, www.mfrl.org/policies/CodeOfEthics.pdf.

Allcott, H., Gentzkow, M. and Yu, C. (2019) Trends in the Diffusion of Misinformation on Social Media, *Research & Politics* **6** (2), 1–8, https://doi.org/10.1177/2053168019848554.

Alowais, S. A., Alghamdi, S. S., Alsuhebany, N., Alqahtani, T., Alshaya, A., Almohareb, S. N., Aldairem, A., Alrashed, M., Bin Saleh, K., Badreldin, H. A., Al Yami, M. S., Al Harbi, S. and Albekairy, A. M. (2023) Revolutionizing Healthcare: The Role of Artificial Intelligence in Clinical Practice, *BMC Medical Education,* **23** (1), 689, https://doi.org/10.1186/s12909-023-04698-z.

Al-Rawi, A. and Zemenchik, K. (2023) Tiktoking COVID-19 with Frontline Workers, *Digital Health,* 8 February, https://doi.org/10.1177/20552076231152766.

Altmetric (2024) www.altmetric.com.

Anderson, P. (2007) What is Web 2.0? Ideas, Technologies and Implications for Education, JISC Technical Report, www.jisc.ac.uk/media/documents/techwatch/tsw0701b.pdf.

Andrews, E. (2019) Who Invented the Internet?, *History,* 28 October, www.history.com/news/who-invented-the-internet.

Anwar, A. A. (2022) A Survey of Semantic Web (Web 3.0), its Applications, Challenges, Future and its Relation with Internet of Things (IoT), *Web Intelligence,* **20** (3),173–202, https://doi.org/10.3233/WEB-210491.

Aspiro Healthcare (2015) *Social Media and Acceptable Use Policy,* www.woodsendmedicalcentre.nhs.uk/social-media-and-acceptable-use-policy.

Atlas, M. C. (2000) The Rise and Fall of the Medical Mediated Searcher, *Bulletin of the Medical Library Association,* **88** (1), 26–35. www.ncbi.nlm.nih.gov/pmc/articles/PMC35195/pdf/i0025-7338-088-01-0026.pdf.

Awurdi, A. P. (2019) Perception of Librarians towards Use of Social Media for Information Service Delivery: A Conceptual Paper, *American International Journal of Multidisciplinary Scientific Research,* **5** (1), 12–17, https://doi.org/10.46281/aijmsr.v5i1.342.

Baker, C. and Hutton, G. (2022) *Rural Mobile Coverage in the UK: Not-Spots and Partial Not-Spots,* House of Commons Library, https://commonslibrary.parliament.uk/research-briefings/sn07069.

Baranowski, T. and Lyons, E. J. (2020) Scoping Review of Pokémon Go: Comprehensive Assessment of Augmented Reality for Physical Activity Change, *Games for Health Journal*, **9** (2), 71–84, https://doi.org/10.1089.g4h.2019.0034.

Barsky, E. (2006) Introducing Web 2.0: Weblogs and Podcasting for Health Librarians, *Journal of the Canadian Health Libraries Association*, **27** (2), https://doi.org/10.5596/c06-013.

Barsky, E. and Giustini, D. (2007) Introducing Web 2.0: Wikis for Health Librarians, *Journal of the Canadian Health Libraries Association*, **28**, 147–50, www.researchgate.net/publication/29734680_Introducing_Web_20_Wikis_for_health_librarians.

Basch, C. H., Fera, J., Pierce, I. and Basch, C. E. (2021) Promoting Mask Use on TikTok: Descriptive, Cross-sectional Study, *JMIR Public Health and Surveillance*, **7** (2), e26392, https://doi.org/10.2196/26392.

Baumgart, D. C. (2005) Personal Digital Assistants in Health Care: Experienced Clinicians in the Palm of your Hand?, *Lancet*, **366** (9492), 1210–22, https://doi.org/10.1016/S0140-6736(05)67484-3.

Baym, N. K. (2015) Social Media and the Struggle for Society, *Social Media + Society*, **1** (1), https://doi.org/10.1177/2056305115580477.

Beattie, A. and Priestley, R. (2021) Fighting COVID-19 with the Team of 5 Million: Aotearoa New Zealand Government Communication During the 2020 Lockdown, *Social Sciences & Humanities Open*, **4** (1), https://doi.org/0.1016/j.ssaho.2021.100209.

Behera, P. K., Jain, S. J. and Kumar, A. (2023) Visual Exploration of Literature Using Connected Papers: A Practical Approach, *Issues in Science and Technology Librarianship*, **104**, https://doi.org/10.29173/istl2760.

Benedict, C., Hahn, A. L., Diefenbach, M. A. and Ford, J. S. (2019) Recruitment via Social Media: Advantages and Potential Biases, *Digital Health*, **5**, https://doi.org/10.1177/20552076198672.

Benetoli, A., Chen, T. F. and Aslani, P. (2018) How Patients' Use of Social Media Impacts their Interactions with Healthcare Professionals, *Patient Education and Counseling*, **101** (3), 439–44, https://doi.org/10.1016/j.pec.2017.08.015.

Berg, S. (2021) *What Doctors Wish Patients Knew about Social Media's Toxic Impact*, American Medical Association, www.ama-assn.org/delivering-care/population-care/what-doctors-wish-patients-knew-about-social-media-s-toxic-impact.

Bernhardt, J. M., Alber, J. and Gold, R. S. (2014) A Social Media Primer for Professionals: Digital Dos and Don'ts, *Health Promotion Practice*, **15**, 168–72, https://doi.org/10.1177/1524839913517235.

Betts, K. R., O'Donoghue, A. C., Aikin, K. J., Kelly, B. J. and Boudewyns, V. (2016) Professional Online Community Membership and Participation among Healthcare Providers: an Extension to Nurse Practitioners and Physician

Assistants, *Journal of the American Association of Nurse Practitioners*, **28**, 639–45, https://doi.org/10.1002/2327-6924.12383.

Bhugaonkar, K., Bhugaonkar, R. and Masne, N. (2022) The Trend of Metaverse and Augmented & Virtual Reality Extending to the Healthcare System, *Cureus*, **14** (9), https://doi.org/10.7759/cureus.29071.

Bianchini, C., Truccolo, I., Bidoli, E. and Mazzocut, M. (2019) Avoiding Misleading Information: A Study of Complementary Medicine Online Information for Cancer Patients, *Library & Information Science Research*, **41** (1), 67–77, https://doi.org/10.1016/j.lisr.2019.02.006.

Blaum, W. E., Jarczweski, A., Balzer, F., Stötzner, P. and Ahlers, O. (2013) Towards Web 3.0: Taxonomies and Ontologies for Medical Education – a Systematic Review, *GMS Zeitschrift für Medizinische Ausbildung*, **30** (1), https://doi.org/10.3205/zma000856.

Blenkinsopp, J. (2008) Bookmarks: Web Blocking – Giving Big Brother a Run for his Money, *He@lth Information on the Internet*, **62**, 10–11.

Boehm, C., Boadu, P., Exley, J., Al-Haboubi, M. and Mays, N. (2023) Public Trust in the Government to Control the Spread of COVID-19 in England After the First Wave – a Longitudinal Analysis, *European Journal of Public Health*, **33** (6), 1155–62, https://doi.org/10.1093/eurpub/ckad148.

Bogost, I. (2022) The Age of Social Media is Ending, *The Atlantic*, www.theatlantic.com/technology/archive/2022/11/twitter-facebook-social-media-decline/672074.

Boreskie, P. E., Chan, T. M., Novak, C., Johnson, A., Wolpaw, J., Ong, A., Priddis, K., Buddhdev, P., Adkins, J., Silverman, J. A., Davis, T. and Siegler, J. E. (2022) Medical Education Blog and Podcast Utilization During the COVID-19 Pandemic, *Cureus*, **14** (3), e23361, https://doi.org/10.7759/cureus.23361.

Borges do Nascimento, I. J., Pizarro, A. B., Almeida, J. M., Azzopardi-Muscat, N., Gonçalves, M. A., Björklund, M. and Novillo-Ortiz, D. (2022) Infodemics and Health Misinformation: A Systematic Review of Reviews, *Bulletin of the World Health Organization*, **100** (9), 544–61, https://doi.org/10.2471/BLT.21.287654.

Boulos, M. N., Hetherington, L. and Wheeler, S. (2007) Second Life: an Overview of the Potential of 3-D Virtual Worlds in Medical and Health Education, *Health Information and Libraries Journal*, **24** (4), 233–45, https://doi.org/10.1111/j.1471-1842.2007.00733.x.

Bour, C., Ahne, A., Schmitz, S., Perchoux, C., Dessenne, C. and Fagherazzi, G. (2021) The Use of Social Media for Health Research Purposes: Scoping Review, *Journal of Medical Internet Research*, **23** (5), e25736, https://doi.org/10.2196/25736.

Boxen, J. L. (2008) Library 2.0: A Review of the Literature, *Reference Librarian*, **49**, 21–34, https://doi.org/10.1080/02763870802103597.

Brainard, J. (2023) Scientific Retractions May Become Easier to Spot as Retraction Watch Finds New Partner, *Science,* www.science.org/content/article/scientific-retractions-may-become-easier-spot-retraction-watch-finds-new-partner.

Bramstedt, K. A. (2020) The Carnage of Substandard Research During the COVID-19 Pandemic: A Call for Quality, *Journal of Medical Ethics,* **46** (12), 803–7, https://doi.org/10.1136/medethics-2020-106494.

Brandon, J. (2022) Here's the Real Problem with Social Media, *Forbes,* www.forbes.com/sites/johnbbrandon/2022/12/14/heres-the-real-problem-with-social-media.

Broady-Preston, J. (2009) Professional Education, Development and Training in a Web 2.0 Environment: a Case Study of the UK, *New Library World,* **110** (5–6), 265–79, https://doi.org/10.1108/03074800910954280.

Brune, C., Agerholm, J. and Liljas, A. (2023) Medical Doctors' Perceptions of the Media Coverage During the Covid-19 Pandemic: A Case Study in Stockholm, *Health Services Insights,* **16,** https://doi.org/10.1177/11786329231222168.

Buck, S. (2020) Hydroxychloroquine Study Flaws Exposed via Social Media Rather than Peer Review, *Arnold Ventures,* 5 June, www.arnoldventures.org/stories/hydroxychloroquine-study-flaws-exposed-via-social-media-rather-than-peer-review.

Cain, J., Linos, E. and Chretien, K. C. (2019) Cyberbullying in Academic Medicine: A Framework for Managing Social Media Attacks, *Academic Medicine,* **94** (5), 626–9, https://doi.org/10.1097/ACM.0000000000002649.

Calvanese Strinati, E., Barbarossa, S., Gonzalez-Jimenez, J. L., Kténas, D., Cassiau, D., Maret, L. and Dehos, C. (2019) 6G: The Next Frontier: From Holographic Messaging to Artificial Intelligence Using Subterahertz and Visible Light Communication, *IEEE Vehicular Technology Magazine,* **14** (3), 42–50, https://doi.org/10.1109/mvt.2019.2921162.

Carboni, A., Woessner, S., Martini, O., Marroquin, N. A. and Waller, J. (2024) Natural Weight Loss or 'Ozempic Face': Demystifying a Social Media Phenomenon, *Journal of Drugs in Dermatology,* **23** (1), 1367–8, https://doi.org/10.36849/JDD.7613.

Carter, B., Ahmed, N., Cassidy, O., Pearson, O., Calcia, M., Mackie, C. and Kalk, N. J. (2024) 'There's More to Life than Staring at a Small Screen': a Mixed Methods Cohort Study of Problematic Smartphone Use and the Relationship to Anxiety, Depression and Sleep in Students Aged 13–16 Years Old in the UK, *BMJ Mental Health,* **27** (1), 5, https://doi.org/10.1136/bmjment-2024-301115.

Carucci, R. (2024) In the Age of AI, Critical Thinking is More Needed Than Ever, *Forbes,* www.forbes.com/sites/roncarucci/2024/02/06/in-the-age-of-ai-critical-thinking-is-more-needed-than-ever.

Casey, M. E. and Savastinuk, L. C. (2006) Library 2.0, *Library Journal,* **131** (14), 40–2.

Ceci, L. (2024) Global TikTok User Age and Gender Distribution 2022, [online] *Statista*, www.statista.com/statistics/1299771/tiktok-global-user-age-distribution.

Céspedes, L. (2021) Latin American Journals and Hegemonic Languages for Academic Publishing in SCOPUS and Web of Science, *Trabalhos Em Linguística Aplicada*, **60** (1), 141–54, https://doi.org/10.1590/010318138901311520201214.

Chamberlain, D., Elcock, M. and Puligari, P. (2015) The Use of Mobile Technology in Health Libraries: A Summary of a UK-Based Survey, *Health Information and Libraries Journal*, **32** (4), 265–75, https://doi.org/10.1111/hir.12116.

Chan, C., Zeng, J. and Schäfer, M. S. (2022) Whose Research Benefits More from Twitter? On Twitter-Worthiness of Communication Research and its Role in Reinforcing Disparities of the Field, *PLOS ONE*, **17** (12), https://doi.org/10.1371/journal.pone.0278840.

Chasca, W., Nerada, S., Zenone, M. and Barbic, S. (2023) TikTok and #OccupationalTherapy: Cross-sectional Study, *JMIR Formative Research*, **7**, https://doi.org/10.2196/45554.

Chavda, J. and Patel, A. (2016) Measuring Research Impact: Bibliometrics, Social Media, Altmetrics, and the BJGP, *British Journal of General Practice*, **66** (642), e59–61, www.doi.org/10.3399/bjgp16X683353.

Chen, S., Wang, B., Wang, X., Shi, K., Cui, W., Liu, Y., Zhang, X. and Wang, Q. (2024) Study on Health Education Methods Based on Rural Residents' Infectious Disease-Specific Health Literacy in Shandong, China, *Medicine (Baltimore)* **103** (32), www.doi.org/10.1097/MD.0000000000039292.

Chewe, P., Sakala, G. and Zulu, Z. (2021) An Exploratory Study on Social Media Literacy Skills Among Librarians at the University Of Zambia, *Zambia Journal of Library & Information Science (ZAJLIS)*, **5** (1), 1–12.

CILIP (Chartered Institute of Library and Information Professionals) (2018) CILIP's Ethical Framework, https://www.cilip.org.uk/page/CILIPEthicsreview.

Coburn, A. (2021) Librarians – The Most Trusted Profession (Almost), The Library Campaign, https://librarycampaign.com/librarians-the-most-trusted-profession-almost.

Cobus-Kuo, L. (2011) Supporting Learners via Web 2.0. In Younger, P. and Morgan, P. (eds), *Using Web 2.0 for Health Information*, 53–65, Facet Publishing.

Collins, G. and Quan-Haase, A. (2012) Social Media and Academic Libraries: Current Trends and Future Challenges, *Proceedings of the American Society for Information Science and Technology*, **49** (1), 1–4, https://doi.org/10.1002/meet.14504901272.

Conde-Caballero, D., Castillo-Sarmiento, C. A., Ballesteros-Yánez, I., Rivero-Jiménez, B. and Mariano-Juárez, L. (2023) Microlearning Through TikTok in Higher Education: an Evaluation of Uses and Potentials, *Education and Information Technologies*, Vol. 29, 2365–85, https://doi.org/10.1007/s10639-023-11904-4.

Connell, R. S. (2009) Academic Libraries, Facebook and MySpace, and Student Outreach: A Survey of Student Opinion, *portal: Libraries and the Academy*, **9** (1), 25–36, https://doi.org/10.1353/pla.0.0036.

Connor, K. L., O'Sullivan, E. D., Marson, L. P., Wigmore, S. J. and Harrison, E. M. (2021) The Future Role of Machine Learning in Clinical Transplantation, *Transplantation*, **105** (4), 723–35, https://doi.org/10.1097/TP.0000000000003424.

Cowles, K., Miller, R. and Suppok, R. (2024) When Seeing Isn't Believing: Navigating Visual Health Misinformation Through Library Instruction, *Medical Reference Services Quarterly*, **43** (1), 44–58, https://doi.org/10.1080/02763869.2024.2290963.

CQC (Care Quality Commission) (2023) Experts by Experience, www.cqc.org.uk/about-us/jobs/experts-experience.

Crotty, B. H. and Mostaghimi, A. (2014) Confidentiality in the Digital Age, *British Medical Journal*, **348**, https://doi.org/10.1136/bmj.g2943.

Cuddy, C., Graham, J. and Morton-Owens, E. G. (2010) Implementing Twitter in a Health Sciences Library, *Medical Reference Services Quarterly*, **29** (4), 320–30, https://doi.org/10.1080/02763869.2010.518915.

Cullinane, C. and Montacute, R. (2020) COVID-19 and Social Mobility Impact Brief #1: School Shutdown, Sutton Trust, www.suttontrust.com/our-research/covid-19-and-social-mobility-impact-brief.

Curry, D. (2025) Microsoft Teams Revenue and Usage Statistics, *Business of Apps*, www.businessofapps.com/data/microsoft-teams-statistics.

Dalmer, N. K. (2017) Questioning Reliability Assessments of Health Information on Social Media, *Journal of the Medical Library Association*, **105** (1), 61–8, https://doi.org/10.5195/jmla.2017.108.

Danbaki, C. A., Mohammed, G. S., Gado, D. S. M. and Ikegwuiro, P. U. (2020) Social Media Use in Libraries and Information Services in Nigerian Tertiary Institutions, *Asian Journal of Research in Computer Science*, **6** (3), 18–26, https://doi.org/10.9734/AJRCOS/2020/V6I330160.

Darko, E. M., Kleib, M. and Olson, J. (2022) Social Media Use for Research Participant Recruitment: Integrative Literature Review, *Journal of Medical Internet Research*, **24** (8), e38015, https://doi.org/10.2196/38015.

Das, S. (2023) NHS Data Breach: Trusts Shared Patient Details with Facebook without Consent, *The Guardian*, www.theguardian.com/society/2023/may/27/nhs-data-breach-trusts-shared-patient-details-with-facebook-meta-without-consent.

Davey, M., Kirchgaessner, S. and Boseley, S. (2020) Surgisphere: Governments and WHO Changed Covid-19 Policy Based on Suspect Data from Tiny US Company, *The Guardian*, www.theguardian.com/world/2020/jun/03/covid-19-surgisphere-who-world-health-organization-hydroxychloroquine.

Davies, C. A., Spence, J. C., Vandelanotte, C., Caperchione, C. M. and Mummery, W. K. (2012) Meta-Analysis of Internet-Delivered Interventions to Increase Physical Activity Levels, *International Journal of Behavioral Nutrition and Physical Activity*, **9** (52), https://10.1186/1479-5868-9-52.

Davis, W. M., Ho, K. and Last, J. (2015) Advancing Social Media in Medical Education, *Canadian Medical Association Journal*, **187**, 549–50, https://doi.org/10.1503/cmaj.141417.

DCMS (2022) Health on the High Street: The Role of Public Libraries, *DCMS Libraries*, https://dcmslibraries.blog.gov.uk/2022/11/16/health-on-the-high-street-the-role-of-public-libraries.

Dean, B. (2022) WhatsApp 2021 User Statistics: How Many People Use WhatsApp?, *Backlinko*, https://backlinko.com/whatsapp-users.

Deb, T. (2024) Social Media in Healthcare Statistics 2024 by Data, Insights, Engagement, *Market.us Media*, https://media.market.us/social-media-in-healthcare-statistics.

De Gagne, J. C., Yamane, S. S., Conklin, J. L., Chang, J. and Kang, H. S. (2018) Social Media Use and Cybercivility Guidelines in U.S. Nursing Schools: A Review of Websites,. *Journal of Professional Nursing*, **34** (1), 35–41, https://doi.org/10.1016/j.profnurs.2017.07.006.

Dehghani, M. and Harris, L. (2023) Current Issues and Status of Mis/Disinformation in the Health Library Context: A Rapid Literature Review, *Journal of Health Information and Libraries Australasia*, **4** (3), 9–25, https://doi.org/10.55999/johila.v4i3.173.

de Jongh, R. and de la Croix, A. (2016) 12 tips to Hear the Voices of Introverts in Medical Education . . . and to Improve the Learning Climate for Everyone, *MedEdPublish*, **10** (107), https://doi.org/10.15694/mep.2021.000107.2.

De-la-Mano, M. (2024) The Historical Development and Current Landscape of Health Library Standards: A Critical Review, *Health Information and Libraries Journal*, **41** (2), 117–35, https://doi.org/10.1111/hir.12530.

Denecke, K., Bamidis, P., Bond, C., Gabarron, E., Househ, M., Lau, A. Y. S., Mayer, M. A., Merolli, M. and Hansen, M. (2018) Ethical Issues of Social Media Usage in Healthcare, *Yearbook of Medical Informatics*, **24** (01), 137–47, https://doi.org/10.15265/IY-2015-001.

Department of Health (2012) *Digital Strategy Leading the Culture Change in Health and Care*, https://assets.publishing.service.gov.uk/media/5a750fbfed915d60d3b90d06/final-report1.pdf.

Devi, S. (2023) Cyber-Attacks on Health-Care Systems, *Lancet Oncology*, **24** (4), e148, https://doi.org/10.1016/S1470-2045(23)00119-5.

Dhingra, M. and Mudgal, R. K. (2019) Historical Evolution of Social Media: An Overview, *International Conference on Advances in Engineering Science*

Management & Technology (ICAESMT) - 2019, Uttaranchal University, Dehradun, India, http://dx.doi.org/10.2139/ssrn.3395665.

Dias da Silva, M., Pereira, A. and Walmsley, A. (2019) Who is Providing Dental Education Content via YouTube?, *British Dental Journal*, **226** (6), 437–40, https://doi.org/10.1038/s41415-019-0046-8.

Divall, P., Camosso-Stefinovic, J. and Baker, R. (2013) The Use of Personal Digital Assistants in Clinical Decision Making by Health Care Professionals: A Systematic Review, *Health Informatics Journal*, **19** (1), 16–28, https://doi.org/10.1177/1460458212446761.

Dixon, S. J. (2024) Topic: Instagram, *Statista*, www.statista.com/topics/1882/instagram.

Dol, J., Tutelman, P. R., Chambers, C. T., Barwick, M., Drake, E. K., Parker, J. A., Parker, R., Benchimol, E. I., George, R. B. and Witteman, H. O. (2019) Health Researchers' Use of Social Media: Scoping Review, *Journal of Medical Internet Research*, **21** (11), e13687, https://doi.org/10.2196/13687.

Dow, B. J., Johnson, A. L., Wang, C. S., Whitson, J. and Menon, T. (2021) The COVID-19 Pandemic and the Search for Structure: Social Media and Conspiracy Theories, *Social and Personality Psychology Compass*, **15** (9), e12636, https://doi.org/10.1111/spc3.12636.

D'Souza, R. S., Hooten, W. M. and Murad, M. H. (2021) A Proposed Approach for Conducting Studies that Use Data from Social Media Platforms, *Mayo Clinic Proceedings*, **96**, 2218–29, https://doi.org/10.1016/j.mayocp.2021.02.010.

Dubale, A. T., Tareke, A. A., Butta, F. W., Shibabaw, A. A., Eniyew, E. B., Ahmed, M. H., Kassie, S. Y., Demsash, A. W., Chereka, A. A., Dube, G. N., Walle, A. D. and Kitil, G. W. (2024) Healthcare Professionals' Willingness to Utilize a Mobile Health Application for Adverse Drug Reaction Reporting in a Limited Resource Setting: An Input for Digital Health, *European Journal of Obstetrics and Gynecology and Reproductive Biology: X*, **23**, 100324, https://doi.org/10.1016/j.eurox.2024.100324.

Duke, V. J. A., Anstey, A., Carter, S., Gosse, N., Hutchens, K. M. and Marsh, J. A. (2017) Social Media in Nurse Education: Utilization and E-Professionalism, *Nurse Education Today*, **57**, 8–13, https://doi.org/10.1016/j.nedt.2017.06.009.

Duong, D. (2021) Should Medical Educators Rethink On-the-Spot Quizzing?, *Canadian Medical Association Journal*, **193** (30), E1182-E1183, https://doi.org/10.1503/cmaj.1095954.

Dwyer, D. E. (2023) The Origins of Severe Acute Respiratory Syndrome-Coronavirus-2, *Seminars in Respiratory and Critical Care Medicine*, **44** (1), 3–7, https://doi.org/10.1055/s-0042-1759564.

eBay (2023) Our History, www.ebayinc.com/company/our-history.

Ebenezer, C. (2017) *'Access Denied'? Barriers for Staff Accessing, Using and Sharing Published Information Online within the National Health Service (NHS) in England: Technology, Risk, Culture, Policy and Practice*, Academia.edu., https://etheses.whiterose.ac.uk/19826/1/CME%20thesis%20v4.0%20White%20Rose%20final%20single%20volume.pdf.

EC-Council (2024) CrowdStrike Incident: Blue Screen of Death, *EC-Council Cybersecurity Exchange*, www.eccouncil.org/cybersecurity-exchange/incident-handling/crowdstrike-incident.

Edinger, A., Valdez, D., Walsh-Buhi, E., Trueblood, J. S., Lorenzo-Luaces, L., Rutter, L. A. and Bollen, J. (2023) Misinformation and Public Health Messaging in the Early Stages of the Mpox Outbreak: Mapping the Twitter Narrative with Deep Learning, *Journal of Medical Internet Research*, **25**, https://doi.org/10.2196/43841.

Ekstrand, M. and Strandberg, L. (2023) Technological Trends in Swedish Medical Libraries, *Health Information and Libraries Journal*, **40** (3), 326–31, https://doi.org/10.1111/hir.12500.

Elad, B. (2024) Skype Statistics 2024 by Country, Devices, Users, Industry and Market Share, *Enterprise Apps Today*, www.enterpriseappstoday.com/stats/skype-statistics.html.

Elliott, K. (2014) Planning for Barriers in Hospital Library Social Media Implementation, *Journal of Hospital Librarianship*, **15** (1), 13–22, https://doi.org/10.1080/15323269.2015.982013.

Ellis, J. T. and Reichel, M. P. (2023) Twitter Trends in #Parasitology Determined by Text Mining and Topic Modelling, *Current Research in Parasitology & Vector Borne Disease*, **4**, https://doi.org/10.1016/j.crpvbd.2023.100138.

Evenstad, L. (2024) NHS Partners with Libraries to Help People Access NHS App, *Computer Weekly*, www.computerweekly.com/news/366608877/NHS-partners-with-libraries-to-help-people-access-NHS-App.

Eysenbach, G. (2009) Infodemiology and Infoveillance: Framework for an Emerging Set of Public Health Informatics Methods to Analyze Search, Communication and Publication Behavior on the Internet, *Journal of Medical Internet Research*, **11** (1), e11, https://doi.org/10.2196/jmir.1157.

Farsi, D. (2021) Social Media and Health Care, Part I: Literature Review of Social Media Use by Health Care Providers, *Journal of Medical Internet Research*, **23** (4), https://doi.org/10.2196/23205.

Fatollahi, J. J., Colbert, J. A., Agarwal, P., Lee, J. L., Lehmann, E. Y., Yuan, N., Lehmann, L. S. and Chretien, K. C. (2020) The Impact of Physician Social Media Behavior on Patient Trust, *AJOB Empirical Bioethics*, **11** (2), 77–82, https://doi.org/10.1080/23294515.2019.1678533.

Fenwick, T. (2014) Social Media and Medical Professionalism: Rethinking the Debate and the Way Forward, *Academic Medicine: Journal of the Association of American Medical Colleges*, **89** (10), 1331–4.

Fernandes, G., Fernandes, M., Vaidya, N., De Souza, P., Plotnikova, E., Geddes, R., Holla, B., Sharma, E., Benegal, V. and Choudhry, V. (2020) Prevalence of Child Maltreatment in India and its Association with Gender, Urbanisation and Policy: A Rapid Review and Meta-Analysis Protocol, *BMJ Open*, **11** (8), e044983, https://doi.org/10.1136/bmjopen-2020-044983.

Fernandez, J. (2009) *A SWOT Analysis for Social Media in Libraries*, University of Maine Library Staff Publications 7, https://digitalcommons.library.umaine.edu/lib_staffpub/7.

Fernández-Luque, L. and Bau, T. (2015) Health and Social Media: Perfect Storm of Information, *Healthcare Informatics Research*, **21** (2), 67–73, https://doi.org/10.4258/hir.2015.21.2.67.

Fisher, J. and Clayton, M. (2012) Who Gives a Tweet: Assessing Patients' Interest in the Use of Social Media for Health Care, *Worldviews on Evidence-Based Nursing*, **9** (2), 100–8, https://doi.org/10.1111/j.1741-6787.2012.00243.x.

Fitzgerald, M. (2019) *Social Media Policy*, East London NHS Foundation Trust, www.elft.nhs.uk/sites/default/files/2022-01/social_media_policy_2.1_2.pdf.

Fouasson-Chailloux, A., Daley, P., Menu, P., Gross, R. and Dauty, M. (2022) Social Media in Health Studies: A Systematic Review of Comparative Learning Methods, *International Journal of Environmental Research and Public Health*, **19** (4), 2205, https://doi.org/10.3390/ijerph19042205.

Fraser, M. (2021) *Policy on the Personal Use of Social Media by Staff*, NHS Eileanan Siar Western Isles, www.wihb.scot.nhs.uk/wp-content/uploads/2020/03/Personal-Use-of-Social-Media-Approved.pdf.

Fu, M. W., Kalaichelvan, A., Liebman, L. S. and Burns, L. E. (2022) Exploring Predoctoral Dental Student Use of YouTube as a Learning Tool for Clinical Endodontic Procedures, *Journal of Dental Education*, **86** (6), 726–35, https://doi.org/10.1002/jdd.12853.

Gabarron, E., Oyeyemi, S. O. and Wynn, R. (2021) COVID-19 Related Misinformation on Social Media: A Systematic Review, *Bulletin of the World Health Organization*, **99**, 455–63A, https://doi.org/10.2471/BLT.20.276782.

Gan, W., Ye, Z., Wan, S. and Yu, P. S. (2023) Web 3.0: The Future of Internet, https://doi.org/10.1145/3543873.3587583.

Garcia-Milian, R., Norton, H. F. and Tennant, M. R. (2012) The Presence of Academic Health Sciences Libraries on Facebook: The Relationship Between Content and Library Popularity, *Medical Reference Services Quarterly*, **31** (2), 171–87, https://doi.org/10.1080/02763869.2012.670588.

Gardois, P., Colombi, N., Grillo, G. and Villanacci, M. C. (2012) Implementation of Web 2.0 Services in Academic, Medical and Research Libraries: A Scoping Review, *Health Information and Libraries Journal*, **29** (2), 90–109, https://doi.org/10.1111/j.1471-1842.2012.00984.x.

Garett, R. and Young, S. D. (2022) The Role of Social Media in Monitoring COVID-19 Vaccine Uptake, *Journal of Evaluation in Clinical Practice*, **28** (4), 650–2, https://doi.org/10.1111/jep.13656.

Garritty, C. and El Emam, K. (2006) Who's Using PDAs? Estimates of PDA Use by Health Care Providers: A Systematic Review of Surveys, *Journal of Medical Internet Research*, **8** (2), e7, https://doi.org/10.2196/jmir.8.2.e7.

Garton, L., Haythornthwaite, C. and Wellman, B. (1997) Studying Online Social Networks, *Journal of Computer-Mediated Communication*, **3** (1), https://doi.org/10.1111/j.1083-6101.1997.tb00062.x

Gent, E. (2021) What Can the Metaverse Learn from Second Life? *IEEE Spectrum*. https://spectrum.ieee.org/metaverse-second-life.

Gerlitz, C. and Helmond, A. (2013) The Like Economy: Social Buttons and the Data-Intensive Web, *New Media & Society*, **15** (8),1348–65, https://doi.org/10.1177/1461444812472322.

Ghalavand, H., Panahi, S. and Sedghi, S. (2020) Opportunities and Challenges of Social Media for Health Knowledge Management: A Narrative Review, *Journal of Education and Health Promotion*, **9**, 144, https://doi.org/10.4103/jehp.jehp_754_19.

Gheshlagh, R. G., Ahsan, M., Jafari, M. and Mahmoodi, H. (2022) Identifying the Challenges of Online Education from the Perspective of University of Medical Sciences Students in the COVID-19 Pandemic: A Q-Methodology-Based Study, *BMC Medical Education*, **22** (1), 895, https://doi.org/10.1186/s12909-022-03980-w.

Gibbs, S. (2016) How Did Email Grow from Messages between Academics to a Global Epidemic? *The Guardian*, www.theguardian.com/technology/2016/mar/07/email-ray-tomlinson-history.

Gillum, S., Williams, N., Herring, P., Walton, D. and Dexter, N. (2018) Encouraging Engagement with Students and Integrating Librarians into the Curriculum through a Personal Librarian Program, *Medical Reference Services Quarterly*, **37** (3), 266–75, https://doi.org/10.1080/02763869.2018.1477710.

Giustini, D. (2010) View of Social Media for Health Librarians, *Journal of the Canadian Health Libraries Association*, **31**, 73–5, https://journals.library.ualberta.ca/jchla/index.php/jchla/article/view/27036/19909.

Giustini, D. (2014) Social Media for Health Librarians, *Journal of the Canadian Health Library Association/Journal de l'Association des bibliothèques de la santé du Canada*, **31**, https://doi.org/10.29173/jchla/jabsc.v31i2.27036.

Glenton, C., Paulsen, E., Agarwal, S., Gopinathan, U., Johansen, M., Kyaddondo, D., Munabi-Babigumira, S., Nabukenya, J., Nakityo, I., Namaganda, R., Namitala, J., Neumark, T., Nsangi, A., Pakenham-Walsh, N. M., Rashidian, A., Royston, G., Sewankambo, N., Tamrat, T. and Lewin, S. (2024) Healthcare Workers' Informal Uses of Mobile Phones and Other Mobile Devices to Support Their

Work: A Qualitative Evidence Synthesis, *Cochrane Database of Systematic Reviews*, **27** (8), https://doi.org/10.1002/14651858.CD015705.pub2.

Global Media Insight (2024) YouTube Statistics 2024 (Users by Country & Demographics), *Official GMI Blog*, www.globalmediainsight.com/blog/youtube-users-statistics.

Goode, D. and Scott, N. (2020) The Use of Social Media (Some) as a Learning Tool in Healthcare Education: An Integrative Review of the Literature, *Nurse Education*, **87**, https://doi.org/10.1016/j.nedt.2020.104357.

Goodson, S. (2012) If You're Not Paying for It, You Become the Product, *Forbes*, www.forbes.com/sites/marketshare/2012/03/05/if-youre-not-paying-for-it-you-become-the-product.

Gopfert, A., Deeny, S. R., Fisher, R. and Stafford, M. (2021) Primary Care Consultation Length by Deprivation and Multimorbidity in England: An Observational Study using Electronic Patient Records, *British Journal of General Practice*, **71** (704), e185-e192, https://doi.org/10.3399/bjgp20X714029.

Gorring, H., Divall, P., Gardner, S., Gray, A., McLaren, A., Snell, L., Thackeray, E., Tocock, A. and Young, G. (2022) NHS Librarians Collaborate to Develop a Search Bank Peer Reviewing and Sharing COVID-19 Searches: An Evaluation, *Health Information and Libraries Journal*, **39** (4), 336–46, https://doi.org/10.1111/hir.12444.

Gotter, A. (2024) The Marketer's Guide to Instagram Hashtags (2024 Update), *Snappa Blog*, https://snappa.com/blog/instagram-hashtags.

Grabeel, K. L., Watson, C. and Wilson, A. Q. (2023) The Significance of the Library's Physical Space: How COVID-19 Impacted a Consumer Health Service, *Journal of the Medical Library Association*, **111** (1–2), 606–11, https://doi.org/10.5195/jmla.2023.1420.

Gross, J. (2012) *Building Your Library Career with Web 2.0*, Chandos Publishing.

Guy, M., Miller, K. S., Barinas, J. and Breazeale, H. (2023) Perspectives of Student Incivility in the Online Learning Environment and Social Media Platforms, *International Journal of Nursing Education Scholarship*, **20** (1), https://doi.org/10.1515/ijnes-2022-0046.

Guyoncourt, S. (2024a) The Countries Where WhatsApp is Banned – and How People are Getting Around It, *inews.co.uk*, https://inews.co.uk/news/world/countries-whatsapp-banned-people-getting-around-it-3033897.

Guyoncourt, S. (2024b) How CrowdStrike Glitch Lifted the Lid on 'Outdated' NHS System, *inews.co.uk*, https://inews.co.uk/news/crowdstrike-glitch-outdated-nhs-system-3193751.

Hanlon, M. (2008) The Mundaneum – the Analog Internet, *New Atlas*, https://newatlas.com/the-mundaneum—the-analog-internet/9491.

Hardey, M. (2008) Public Health and Web 2.0, *Journal of the Royal Society for the Promotion of Health*, **128**, 181–9, https://doi.org/10.1177/1466424008092228.

Harish, V., Ackery, A., Grant, K., Jamieson, T. and Mehta, S. (2023) Cyberattacks on Canadian Health Information Systems, *Canadian Medical Association Journal*, https://doi.org/10.1503/cmaj.230436.

Harrow, A., Marks, L. A., Schneider, D., Lyubechansky, A., Aaronson, E., Kysh, L. and Harrington, M. (2019) Hospital Library Closures and Consolidations: A Case Series, *Journal of the Medical Library Association*, **107** (2), https://doi.org/10.5195/jmla.2019.520.

Haynes, B. and Haines, A. (1998) Barriers and Bridges to Evidence Based Clinical Practice, *British Medical Journal*, **317** (7153), 273–6, https://doi.org/10.1136/bmj.317.7153.273.

HCPC (Health and Care Professions Council) (2022) Using Social Media Wisely, www.hcpc-uk.org/news-and-events/blog/2022/using-social-media-wisely.

He, D., Zhao, S., Li, Y., Cao, P., Gao, D., Lou, Y. and Yang, L. (2020) Comparing COVID-19 and the 1918–19 Influenza Pandemics in the United Kingdom, *International Journal of Infectious Diseases*, **98**, 67–70, https://doi.org/10.1016/j.ijid.2020.06.075.

Health Education England (2019) *Preparing the Healthcare Workforce to Deliver the Digital Future: An Independent Report on Behalf of the Secretary of State for Health and Social Care*, https://topol.hee.nhs.uk/wp-content/uploads/HEE-Topol-Review-2019-printable.pdf.

Hendrix, D., Chiarella, D., Hasman, L., Murphy, S. and Zafron, M. L. (2009) Use of Facebook in Academic Health Sciences Libraries, *Journal of the Medical Library Association*, **97** (1), 44–7, https://doi.org/10.3163/1536-5050.97.1.008.

Henner, T. A. (2023) Implementing a Personal Librarian Program to Rebuild Connections with Medical Students, *Medical Reference Services Quarterly*, **42** (2),140–52, https://doi.org/10.1080/02763869.2023.2194146.

Herd Digital (2022) Facebook Statistics You Must Know in 2022, https://herd.digital/blog/facebook-statistics-2022.

Hern, A. (2024) Twitter Usage in the US 'Fallen by a Fifth' since Elon Musk's Takeover, *The Guardian*, www.theguardian.com/technology/2024/mar/26/twitter-usage-in-us-fallen-by-a-fifth-since-elon-musks-takeover.

Herrero-Diz, P. and López-Rufino, C. (2021) Libraries Fight Disinformation: An Analysis of Online Practices to Help Users' Generations in Spotting Fake News, *Societies*, **11** (4), 133, https://doi.org/10.3390/soc11040133.

Hinchcliffe, D. (2006) All We Got Was Web 1.0, When Tim Berners-Lee Actually Gave us Web 2.0, *On Digital Strategy*, https://dionhinchcliffe.com/2006/09/04/all-we-got-was-web-1-0-when-tim-berners-lee-actually-gave-us-web-2-0.

Hoernke, K., Djellouli, N., Andrews, L., Lewis-Jackson, S., Manby, L., Martin, S., Vanderslott, S. and Vindrola-Padros, C. (2021) Frontline Healthcare Workers' Experiences with Personal Protective Equipment During the COVID-19 Pandemic in the UK: A Rapid Qualitative Appraisal, *British Medical Journal Open*, **11** (1), https://doi.org/10.1136/bmjopen-2020-046199.

Holmberg, K. J. (2024) Altmetrics for Information Professionals: Past, Present and Future, Chandos.

Househ, M. (2013) The Use of Social Media in Healthcare: Organizational, Clinical, and Patient Perspectives, *Studies in Health Technology and Informatics*, **183**, 244–8, https://doi.org/10.3233/978-1-61499-203-5-244.

Howarth, J. (2022) Top 20 New Social Media Networks (Mar 2023), *Exploding Topics*, 16 May, https://explodingtopics.com/blog/new-social-media-networks.

Hughes B., Joshi I., Lemonde, H. and Wareham J. (2009) Junior Physician's Use of Web 2.0 for Information Seeking and Medical Education: A Qualitative Study, *International Journal of Medical Informatics*, **78** (10) 645–55, https://doi.org/10.1016/j.ijmedinf.2009.04.008.

Hull York Medical School (2019) *Our Partners*, www.hyms.ac.uk/about/our-partners.

Humphreys, S. (2019) Tweeting into the Void?: Creating a UK Library Twitter List and Analysing Best Practice – Successes and Myths, *Insights*, **32** (1), https://insights.uksg.org/articles/10.1629/uksg.471.

Hurt, E. and Grundy, D. (2024) Internal and External Partnerships. In Walton, G., Johnson, F., Stewart, D., Young, G. and Case Wyatt, H. (eds) *Introduction to Healthcare Knowledge and Library Services*, 85–101, Facet Publishing.

Hussain, F. (2012) E-Learning 3.0 = E-Learning 2.0 + Web 3.0? *IOSR Journal of Research & Method in Education*, **3** (3), 39–47, https://doi.org/10.9790/7388-0333947.

Iflaifel, M., Hall, C. L., Green, H. R., Willis, A., Rennick Egglestone, S., Juszczak, E., Townsend, M., Martin, J. and Sprange, K. (2023) Widening Participation – Recruitment Methods in Mental Health Randomised Controlled Trials: A Qualitative Study, *BMC Medical Research Methodology*, **23** (1), https://doi.org/10.1186/s12874-023-02032-1.

Imbens, G. W. and Kalyanaraman, K. (2009) Optimal Bandwidth Choice for the Regression Discontinuity Estimator, IZA Discussion Paper No. 3995, https://doi.org/10.2139/ssrn.1351159.

Internet Society (1997) *Brief History of the Internet*, www.internetsociety.org/internet/history-internet/brief-history-internet.

Iwendi, C., Mohan, S., Khan, S., Ibeke, E., Ahmadian, A. and Ciano, T. (2022) Covid-19 Fake News Sentiment Analysis, *Computers and Electrical Engineering*, **101**,107967, https://doi.org/10.1016/j.compeleceng.2022.107967.

Jacob, C., Sanchez-Vazquez, A. and Ivory, C. (2020) Social, Organizational, and Technological Factors Impacting Clinicians' Adoption of Mobile Health Tools:

Systematic Literature Review, *JMIR Mhealth and Uhealth*, **8** (2), https://doi.org/10.2196/15935.

Jaeger, P. T. and Greene Taylor, N. (2021) Arsenals of Lifelong Information Literacy: Educating Users to Navigate Political and Current Events Information in World of Ever-Evolving Misinformation, *The Library Quarterly*, **91** (1), 19–31, https://doi.org/10.1086/711632.

Jahagirdar, V., Rama, K., Soppari, P. and Kumar, M. V. (2021) Mobile Phones: Vital Addiction or Lethal Addiction? Mobile Phone Usage Patterns and Assessment of Mobile Addiction among Undergraduate Medical Students in Telangana, India, *Journal of Addiction*, https://doi.org/10.1155/2021/8750650.

Jeyaraman, M., Ramasubramanian, S., Kumar, S., Jeyaraman, N., Selvaraj, P., Nallakumarasamy, A., Bondili, S. K. and Yadav, S. (2023) Multifaceted Role of Social Media in Healthcare: Opportunities, Challenges, and the Need for Quality Control, *Cureus*, **15** (5), https://doi.org/10.7759/cureus.39111.

Jones, K., Wilson-Keates, B. and Melrose, S. (2024) Using Social Media to Recruit Research Participants: A Literature Review, *Nurse Researcher*, **32** (1), 28–34, https://doi.org/10.7748/nr.2023.e1859.

Joo, S., Choi, N. and Baek, T. H. (2018) Library Marketing via Social Media: the Relationships between Facebook Content and User Engagement in Public Libraries, *Online Information Review*, **42** (6), 940–55, https://doi.org/10.1108/OIR-10-2017-0288.

Jordan, K. (2019) From Social Networks to Publishing Platforms: A Review of the History and Scholarship of Academic Social Network Sites, *Frontiers in Digital Humanities*, **6**, https://doi.org/10.3389/fdigh.2019.00005.

Joseph, A. M., Fernandez, V., Kritzman, S., Eaddy, I., Cook, O. M., Lambros, S., Jara Silva, C. E., Arguelles, D., Abraham, C., Dorgham, N., Gilbert, Z. A., Chacko, L., Hirpara, R. J., Mayi, B. S. and Jacobs, R. J. (2022) COVID-19 Misinformation on Social Media: A Scoping Review, *Cureus*, **14** (4), https://doi.org/10.7759/cureus.24601.

Just, M. L. (2003) New Roles, *Medical Reference Services Quarterly*, **22** (4), 65–73, https://doi.org/10.1300/J115v22n04_07.

Kamadjeu, R. (2019) English: the Lingua Franca of Scientific Research, *Lancet Global Health*, **7** (9), www.thelancet.com/journals/langlo/article/PIIS2214-109X(19)30258-X/fulltext.

Kamel Boulos, M. N. and Wheeler, S. (2007) The Emerging Web 2.0 Social Software: An Enabling Suite of Sociable Technologies in Health and Health Care Education, *Health Information and Libraries Journal*, **24** (1), 2–23, https://doi.org/10.1111/j.1471-1842.2007.00701.x.

Kanchan, S. and Gaidhane, A. (2023) Social Media Role and Its Impact on Public Health: A Narrative Review, *Cureus*, **15** (1), https://doi.org/10.7759/cureus.33737.

Karki, M., El Asmar, M. L., Sasco, E. R. and El-Osta, A. (2024) Public Libraries to Promote Public Health and Wellbeing: A Cross-Sectional Study of Community-Dwelling Adults, *BMC Public Health*, **24** (1), 1226, https://doi.org/10.1186/s12889-024-18535-5.

Kauffman, L., Weisberg, E. M. and Fishman, E. K. (2022) TikTok for Radiology Education: Is Now the Right Time? *Current Problems in Diagnostic Radiology*, **51** (6), 826–8.

Kemp, S. (2024) Internet Use in 2024, *DataReportal – Global Digital Insights*, https://datareportal.com/reports/digital-2024-deep-dive-the-state-of-internet-adoption.

Kendrick, K. T., Leaver, E. and Tritt, D. (2013) Link up the Sticks: Access and Barriers to Professional Development for Small and Rural Academic Librarians, *Codex: The Journal of the Louisiana Chapter of the ACRL*, **2** (3), 38–77, https://doi.org/10.1067/j.cpradiol.2022.06.001.

Khanagar, S. B., Alolayan, S. L., Alobaid, T. A., Alharbi, A. A., Alazaz, N. N. and Alanazi, M. H. (2022) Use of YouTube as a Learning Modality for Clinical Procedures among Dental Students in Riyadh, Saudi Arabia – a Cross-Sectional Study, *Applied Sciences*, **12** (23), https://doi.org/10.3390/app122311977.

Kim, J. (2023) Have Academic Library Staffing Numbers Really Declined That Much over the Past Decade? *Inside Higher Ed*, www.insidehighered.com/blogs/learning-innovation/have-academic-library-staffing-numbers-really-declined-much-over-past.

Kind, T. (2015) Professional Guidelines for Social Media Use: A Starting Point, *AMA Journal of Ethics*, **17**, 441–7, https://journalofethics.ama-assn.org/article/professional-guidelines-social-media-use-starting-point/2015-05.

Kiran, F. (2022) Health Information Sharing on Facebook: An Exploratory Study on COVID-19, *Global Journal for Management and Administrative Sciences*, **3** (1), 63–74, https://doi.org/10.46568/gjmas.v3i1.101.

Kirkpatrick, C. E. and Lawrie, L. L. (2024) TikTok as a Source of Health Information and Misinformation for Young Women in the United States: Survey Study, *JMIR Infodemiology*, **4**, https://doi.org/10.2196/54663.

Koning, I. M., van den Eijnden, R. J. J. M. and Vossen, H. G. M. (2024) From Greenwashing to Screenwashing? *Journal of Behavioral Addictions*, **13** (1), 1–5, https://doi.org/10.1556/2006.2023.00084.

Kordzadeh, N. and Young, D. K. (2018) Exploring Hospitals' Use of Facebook: Thematic Analysis, *Journal of Medical Internet Research*, **20** (5), www.jmir.org/2018/5/e190.

Kraushaar, J. and Bohnet-Joschko, S. (2023) Prevalence and Patterns of Mobile Device Usage among Physicians in Clinical Practice: A Systematic Review, *Health Informatics Journal*, **29** (2), https://doi.org/10.1177/14604582231169296.

Krawczyk, F. and Kulczycki, E. (2021) How is Open Access Accused of Being Predatory? The Impact of Beall's Lists of Predatory Journals on Academic Publishing, *The Journal of Academic Librarianship*, **47** (2), 102271, https://doi.org/10.1016/j.acalib.2020.102271.

Lacey Bryant, S., Bridgen, R., Hopkins, E., McLaren, C. and Stewart, D. (2022) NHS Knowledge and Library Services in England in the Digital Age, *Health Information and Libraries Journal,* **39** (4), 385–91, https://doi.org/10.1111/hir.12457.

Lafferty, N. (2013) *NHS-HE Connectivity Project Web 2.0 and Social Media in Education and Research,* https://community.jisc.ac.uk/system/files/515/NHF_Web2%200SoMEinEdResearch_May2013_final.pdf.

Lambert, K. M., Barry, P. and Stokes, G. (2012) Risk Management and Legal Issues with the Use of Social Media in the Healthcare Setting, *Journal of Healthcare Risk Management,* **31**, 41–7, https://doi.org/10.1002/jhrm.20103.

Lancaster, R., Sanchez, M., Maxwell, K. and Medley, R. (2022) Original Research: TikTok's 'Dancing Nurses' During the COVID-19 Pandemic: A Content Analysis, *American Journal of Nursing,* **122** (12), 24–31, https://doi.org/10.1097/01.NAJ.0000901844.48930.c8.

Langer, S. L., Castro, F. G., Chen, A. C., Davis, K. C., Joseph, R. P., Kim, W. S., Larkey, L., Lee, R. E., Petrov, M. E., Reifsnider, E., Youngstedt, S. D. and Shaibi, G. Q. (2021) Recruitment and Retention of Underrepresented and Vulnerable Populations to Research, *Public Health Nursing,* **38** (6),1102–15, https://doi.org/10.1111/phn.12943.

Latif, M. Z., Hussain, I., Saeed, R., Qureshi, M. A. and Maqsood, U. (2019) Use of Smart Phones and Social Media in Medical Education: Trends, Advantages, Challenges and Barriers, *Acta Informatica Medica,* **27**, 133–8, https://doi.org/10.5455/aim.2019.27.133-138.

Laurent, M. R. and Vickers, T. J. (2009) Seeking Health Information Online: Does Wikipedia Matter? *Journal of the American Medical Informatics Association,* **16** (4), 471–9, https://doi.org/10.1197/jamia.M3059.

Law, R. W., Kanagasingam, S. and Choong, K. A. (2021) Sensationalist Social Media Usage by Doctors and Dentists During Covid-19, *Digital Health,* **29** (7), https://doi.org/10.1177/20552076211028034.

Lawson, L., Barros, R. D. M., Evans, J. and Saleem, W. (2023) Being a 'Teams' Player: A Quality Improvement Project Expanding the Role of Microsoft Teams to Improve Communication and Efficiency of Junior Doctors in a Ward-Based Hospital Setting, *Future Health Journal,* **10** (Suppl. 3), 89–90, https://doi.org/10.7861/fhj.10-3-s89.

Leman, H. (2012) Social Media in Healthcare: Connect, Communicate, Collaborate, *Journal of the Medical Library Association,* **100** (2), 148–9, https://doi.org/10.3163/1536-5050.100.2.018.

Lentzen, M. P., Huebenthal, V., Kaiser, R., Kreppel, M., Zoeller, J. E. and Zirk, M. (2022) A Retrospective Analysis of Social Media Posts Pertaining to COVID-19 Vaccination Side Effects, *Vaccine*, **40** (1), 43–51, https://doi.org/10.1016/j.vaccine.2021.11.052.

Li, S., Zeng, Y., Guo, S. and Zhuang, X. (2019) Investigation and Analysis of Research Support Services in Academic Libraries, *Electronic Library*, **37** (2), 281–301, https://doi. org/10.1108/EL-06-2018-0125.

Li, B., Liu, M., Liu, J., Zhang, Y., Yang, W. and Xie, L. (2024) Quality Assessment of Health Science-Related Short Videos on TikTok: A Scoping Review, *International Journal of Medical Informatics*, **186**, https://doi.org/10.1016/j.ijmedinf.2024.105426.

Liang, B. A. and Mackey, T. K. (2012) Online Availability and Safety of Drugs in Shortage: A Descriptive Study of Internet Vendor Characteristics, *Journal of Medical Internet Research*, **14** (1), e27, https://doi.org/10.2196/jmir.1999.

Liang, S. T., Liang, L. T. and Rosen, J. M. (2021) COVID-19: A Comparison to the 1918 Influenza and How We Can Defeat it, *Postgraduate Medical Journal*, **97** (1147), 273–4, https://doi.org/10.1136/postgradmedj-2020-139070.

Lim, V. W., Lim, R. L., Tan, Y. R., Soh, A. S., Tan, M. X., Othman, N. B., Borame Dickens, S., Thein, T. L., Lwin, M. O., Ong, R. T., Leo, Y. S., Lee, V. J. and Chen, M. I. (2021) Government Trust, Perceptions of COVID-19 and Behaviour Change: Cohort Surveys, Singapore, *Bulletin of the World Health Organization*, **99** (2), 92–101, https://doi.org/10.2471/BLT.20.269142.

Liu, Y., Amin, R. and Stemmler, H. (2024) Digital Adoption: Accelerating Postpandemic, yet a Widening Divide in World Bank (2024) Digital Progress and Trends Report 2023, https://openknowledge.worldbank.org/entities/publication/7617f89d-2276-413d-b0a7-e31e7527d6af.

Lowais, S. A., Alghamdi, S. S., Alsuhebany, N., Alqahtani, T., Alshaya, A. I., Almohareb, S. N., Aldairem, A., Alrashed, M., Bin Saleh, K., Badreldin, H. A., Al Yami, M. S., Al Harbi, S. and Albekairy, A. M. (2023) Revolutionizing Healthcare: the Role of Artificial Intelligence in Clinical Practice, *BMC Medical Education*, **23** (1), 689, https://doi.org/10.1186/s12909-023-04698-z.

Lund, B. D., Khan, D. and Yuvaraj, M. (2024) ChatGPT in Medical Libraries, Possibilities and Future Directions: An Integrative Review, *Health Information and Libraries Journal*, **41** (1), 4–15, https://doi.org/10.1111/hir.12518.

Luo, T. and Hostetler, K. (2020) Making Professional Development More Social: A Systematic Review of Librarians' Professional Development through Social Media, *Journal of Academic Librarianship*, **46** (5), https://doi.org/10.1016/j.acalib.2020.102193.

Macdonald, G. (2014) 5 Ways Libraries Are Using Social Media, *CILIP: The Library and Information Association*, www.cilip.org.uk/news/475701/5-ways-libraries-are-using-social-media.htm.

Maggio, L. A., Willinsky, J. M., Costello, J. A., Skinner, N. A., Martin, P. C. and Dawson, J. E. (2020) Integrating Wikipedia Editing into Health Professions Education: A Curricular Inventory and Review of the Literature, *Perspectives on Medical Education*, **9** (6), 333–42, https://doi.org/10.1007/s40037-020-00620-1.

Mahdavi Ardestani, S. F., Adibi, S., Golshan, A. and Sadeghian, P. (2023) Factors Influencing the Effectiveness of E-Learning in Healthcare: A Fuzzy ANP Study, *Healthcare (Basel)*, **11** (14), 2035, https://doi.org/10.3390/healthcare11142035.

Maheshwari, S. and Holpuch, A. (2024) Why TikTok Faces a U.S. Ban, and What's Next?, *The New York Times*, www.nytimes.com/article/tiktok-ban.html.

Malhotra S. (2023) TikTok Surgery Reignites Worries over Doctors and Social Media, *British Medical Journal*, **380**, 499, https://doi.org/10.1136/bmj.p499.

Malik, R. (2019) Using Social Media for Student Engagement: A Study of Two New Zealand Academic Libraries, Master's project, Victoria University of Wellington, *Te Herenga Waka*, http://hdl.handle.net/10063/8201.

Mamdapur, G. M. N., Patel, A. K. and Gupta, B. M. (2022) The Impact of Social Media and Libraries: A Global Analysis of Publications. In Krishnamurthy, M., Ramesha, B. and Subhash, R. B. (eds), *International Conference on Emerging Digital Library Platforms: Shaping Digital Transformation and National Data Exchange 2022*, 588–600, http://dx.doi.org/10.2139/ssrn.4343645.

Marr, B. (2024) The Metaverse and Its Dark Side: Confronting the Reality of Virtual Rape, *Forbes*, www.forbes.com/sites/bernardmarr/2024/01/16/the-metaverse-and-its-dark-side-confronting-the-reality-of-virtual-rape.

Marshal, M., Niranjan, V., Spain, E., MacDonagh, J., O'Doherty, J., O'Connor, R. and O'Regan, A. (2012) 'Doctors Can't be Doctors All of the Time': A Qualitative Study of How General Practitioners and Medical Students Negotiate Public Professional and Private–Personal Realms using Social Media, *British Medical Journal Open*, **11**, https://doi.org/10.1136/bmjopen-2020-047991.

McCallum, S. (2022) Meta Settles Cambridge Analytica Scandal Case for $725m, *BBC News*, www.bbc.co.uk/news/technology-64075067.

McCormick, C. and Pickard, A. J. (2013) An Evaluation on the Effectiveness of Web 2.0 Startpages (Netvibes & Pageflakes) Within NHS Libraries, *Health Information and Libraries Journal*, **30** (2), 155–60, https://doi.org/10.1111/hir.12029.

McIntyre, K. E. (2014) The Evolution of Social Media from 1969 to 2013: A Change in Competition and a Trend Toward Complementary, Niche Sites, *The Journal of Social Media in Society*, **3** (2), https://thejsms.org/index.php/JSMS/article/view/89.

Mehrazar, M., Kling, C. C., Lemke, S., Mazarakis, A. and Peters, I. (2018) Can We Count on Social Media Metrics? First Insights into the Active Scholarly Use of Social Media, *Proceedings of the 10th ACM Conference on Web Science* (WebSci '18), 215–19, https://doi.org/10.1145/3201064.3201101.

Mejova, Y. and Kalimeri, K. (2020) Advertisers Jump on Coronavirus Bandwagon: Politics, News, and Business, *ArXiv:2003.00923 [cs:SI]*, https://arxiv.org/abs/2003.00923.

Meth, J. (2019) The Tragic Side of Tide Pods, *Fortune*, https://fortune.com/longform/tide-pod-poisoning-injuries-epidemic.

Meyer, M., Shoukfeh, R., Turk, D. and Potts, G. (2023) Misinformation about Monkeypox on TikTok, *Skinmed*, **21** (4), 248–51.

Miller, D., Costa, E., Haynes, N., McDonald, T., Nicolescu, R., Sinanan, J., Spyer, J., Venkatraman, S. and Wang, X. (2016) How the World Changed Social Media, UCL Press, https://doi.org/10.14324/111.9781910634493.

Miller, M. J. (2014) 25 Years Later: How a 'Mesh' Turned Into the World Wide Web, *UKPCMag*, https://uk.pcmag.com/opinion/10449/25-years-later-how-a-mesh-turned-into-the-world-wide-web.

Milmo, D. and Hawkins, A. (2023) 'The Everything App': Why Elon Musk Wants X to Be a WeChat for the West, *The Guardian*, www.theguardian.com/media/2023/jul/29/elon-musk-wechat-twitter-rebranding-everything-app-for-west.

Ming, S., Han, J., Li, M., Liu, Y., Xie, K. and Lei, B. (2023) TikTok and Adolescent Vision Health: Content and Information Quality Assessment of the Top Short Videos Related to Myopia, *Frontiers in Public Health*, **10**, https://doi.org/10.3389/fpubh.2022.1068582.

Minhaj, F. and Leonard, J. (2021) Dangers of the Tiktok Benadryl Challenge, *Contemporary PEDS Journal*, **38**, www.contemporarypediatrics.com/view/dangers-of-the-tiktok-benadryl-challenge.

Minocha, S. (2009) A Case Study-Based Investigation of Students' Experiences with Social Software Tools, *New Review of Hypermedia and Multimedia*, **15** (3), 245–65, https://doi.org/10.1080/13614560903494320.

Mistry, P. (2024) Is the Spring Budget a Game Changer for NHS Technology? The King's Fund, www.kingsfund.org.uk/insight-and-analysis/blogs/spring-budget-game-changer-nhs-technology.

Mistry, P., Lindsay, T. and Patterson, M. (2024) Siloed, Unsupported and Hindered – The Reality of Innovation in the NHS and Social Care, The King's Fund, www.kingsfund.org.uk/insight-and-analysis/blogs/siloed-unsupported-hindered-innovation-nhs-social-care.

Mobasheri, M. H., King, D., Johnston, M., Gautama, S., Purkayastha, S. and Darzi, A. (2015) The Ownership and Clinical Use of Smartphones by Doctors and Nurses in the UK: A Multicentre Survey Study, *BMJ Innovations*, **1**, 174–81, https://doi.org/10.1136/bmjinnov-2015-000062.

Mohammadi, E., Thelwall, M., Kwasny, M. and Holmes, K. L. (2018) Academic Information on Twitter: A User Survey, *PLoS One*, **13** (5), e0197265, https://doi.org/10.1371/journal.pone.0197265.

Mon, L. (2015) *Social Media and Library Services*, Morgan & Claypool.

Moreman, R. (2020) *Social Media Policy*, University Hospitals Dorset NHS Foundation Trust, www.uhd.nhs.uk/uploads/about/docs/policies/corporate/Social-Media-Policy.pdf.

Morgan, A. B. (2019) Using Contingent Medical Librarians to Address Workforce Staffing Dilemmas, *Medical Reference Services Quarterly*, **38** (4), 376–86, https://doi.org/10.1080/02763869.2019.1657732.

Morgen, E. B. (2003) Implementing PDA technology in a Medical Library: Experiences in a Hospital Library and an Academic Medical Center Library, *Medical Reference Services Quarterly*, **22** (1), 11–19, https://doi.org/10.1300/J115v22n01_02.

Morse, E., Odigie, E., Gillespie, H. and Rameau, A. (2024) The Readability of Patient-Facing Social Media Posts on Common Otolaryngologic Diagnoses, *Otolaryngology – Head and Neck Surgery*, **170** (4), 1051–8, https://doi.org/10.1002/ohn.584.

Morse, G. (2003) The Science Behind Six Degrees, *Harvard Business Review*, https://hbr.org/2003/02/the-science-behind-six-degrees.

Motta, M. and Stecula, D. (2021) Quantifying the Effect of Wakefield et al. (1998) on Skepticism about MMR Vaccine Safety in the U.S., *PLoS One*, **16** (8), https://doi.org/10.1371/journal.pone.0256395.

Mouelhi, Y., Alessandrini, M., Pauly, V., Dussol, B. and Gentile, S. (2017) Internet and Social Network Users' Profiles in Renal Transplant Recipients in France, *BMC Nephrology*, **18** (1), 259, https://doi.org/10.1186/s12882-017-0670-y.

Moulds, A. and Horton, T. (2023) What Do Technology and AI Mean for the Future of Work in Health Care?, *The Health Foundation*, www.health.org.uk/publications/long-reads/what-do-technology-and-ai-mean-for-the-future-of-work-in-health-care.

Müller, S. and Koschate, A.-C. (2012) Second Life: neuer Markt oder vergänglicher Hype? *Social Science Open Access Repository*, www.ssoar.info/ssoar/handle/document/37804.

Murad, A., Hyde, N., Chang, S., Lederman, R., Bosua, R., Pirotta, M., Audehm, R., Yates, C. J., Briggs, A. M., Gorelik, A., Chiang, C. and Wark, J. D. (2019) Quantifying Use of a Health Virtual Community of Practice for General

Practitioners' Continuing Professional Development: A Novel Methodology and Pilot Evaluation, *Journal of Medical Internet Research,* **21** (11), https://doi.org/10.2196/14545.

Naeem, S. B. and Bhatti, R. (2020) The Covid-19 'Infodemic': A New Front for Information Professionals, *Health Information and Libraries Journal,* **37** (3), 233–39, https://doi.org/10.1111/hir.12311.

Nasar, M. (2023) Web 3.0: A Review and its Future, *International Journal of Computer Applications,* **185** (10), 41–6, https://doi.org/10.5120/ijca2023922776.

National Awareness Days (2024) National Awareness Days Events Calendar 2024, www.awarenessdays.com.

Naughton, J. (2016) The Evolution of the Internet: From Military Experiment to General Purpose Technology, *Journal of Cyber Policy,* **1** (1), 5–28, https://doi.org/10.1080/23738871.2016.1157619.

Nebeker, C., Lagare, T., Takemoto, M., Lewars, B., Crist, K., Bloss, C. S. and Kerr, J. (2016) Engaging Research Participants to Inform the Ethical Conduct of Mobile Imaging, Pervasive Sensing, and Location Tracking Research, *Translational Behavioral Medicine,* **6**, 577–86, https://doi.org/10.1007/s13142-016-0426-4.

Neilson, C. J. (2016) What Do Health Libraries Tweet About? A Content Analysis, *Partnership: The Canadian Journal of Library and Information Practice and Research,* **11** (1), https://doi.org/10.21083/partnership.v11i1.3661.

Nelson, B. M. and Schultz, P. L. (2019) The Tide Pod Challenge: Responding to The Threat of Viral Internet Phenomena, *Journal of Case Studies,* **37** (2).

Nestor, M. S., Fischer, D. L., Arnold, D., Berman, B. and Del Rosso, J. Q. (2020) Rethinking the Journal Impact Factor and Publishing in the Digital Age, *Journal of Clinical and Aesthetic Dermatology,* **13** (1), 12–17, www.ncbi.nlm.nih.gov/pmc/articles/PMC7028381/pdf/jcad_13_1_12.pdf.

Ng, R. and Indran, N. (2023) Granfluencers on TikTok: Factors Linked to Positive Self-Portrayals of Older Adults on Social Media, *PLoS One,* **18** (2), https://doi.org/10.1371/journal.pone.0280281.

NHS Digital (2022) Blocking Web Malicious Content (6.2.5), NHS England Digital, https://digital.nhs.uk/cyber-and-data-security/guidance-and-assurance/data-security-and-protection-toolkit-assessment-guides/guide-6—-responding-to-incidents/blocking-web-malicious-content.

NHS Employers (2025) Calendar of National Campaigns, www.nhsemployers.org/events/calendar-national-campaigns.

NHS England (2022) *Health and Digital Literacy Partnership Provides Local Learning for Better Health,* https://library.nhs.uk/our-news.

NHS England (2023a) *Social Media,* https://www.england.nhs.uk/long-read/social-media.

NHS England (2023b) *NHS Long Term Workforce Plan,* www.england.nhs.uk/publication/nhs-long-term-workforce-plan.

NHS England (2024) *NHS Library and Knowledge Staff Ratios Policy – Knowledge and Library Services*, https://library.nhs.uk/employer-leaders/staff-ratios-policy.

Niburski, K. and Niburski, O. (2020) Impact of Trump's Promotion of Unproven COVID-19 Treatments and Subsequent Internet Trends: Observational Study, *Journal of Medical Internet Research*, **22** (11), https://doi.org/10.2196/20044.

Norman, N. (2011) *Mobile Learning for the NHS: Research Report*, NHS South Central Strategic Health Authority and Epic Learning Group, www.workforce.southcentral.nhs.uk/pdf/Mobile_learning_NHS_Research_Final_Report.pdf.

O'Doherty, D., Dromey, M., Lougheed, J., Hannigan, A., Last, J. and McGrath, D. (2018) Barriers and Solutions to Online Learning in Medical Education – an Integrative Review, *BMC Medical Education*, **18** (1),130, https://doi.org/10.1186/s12909-018-1240-0.

OECD (2018) Sweden in the Digital Transformation: Opportunities and Challenges. In *OECD Reviews of Digital Transformation: Going Digital in Sweden*, 17–33, https://doi.org/10.1787/9789264302259-3-en.

Omini, E. U. and Osuolale, K. A. (2019) Utilization of Social Media Platforms by Librarians for Promoting Library Resources and Services in Nigerians' Tertiary Institutions in Cross River State, *Global Journal of Educational Research*, **18** (1), 1–8, https://doi.org/10.4314/gjedr.v18i1.1.

O'Reilly, T. (2005) *What Is Web 2.0*, www.oreilly.com/pub/a/web2/archive/what-is-web-20.html.

O'Reilly, T. and Battelle, J. (2009) *Web Squared: Web 2.0 Five Years On*, https://eric-blue.com/projects/docbrowser/docs/Technology/OReilly-Web-Squared-Whitepaper-2009.pdf.

Ortutay, B. (2023) A Year after Musk Takeover, X Struggles with Usage Decline and Misinformation, *AP News*, https://apnews.com/article/twitter-x-elon-musk-takeover-anniversary-ac2cb6419d93d64086cc9ad980c5a57a.

Ostrovsky, A. M. and Chen, J. R. (2020) TikTok and its Role in COVID-19 Information Propagation, *Journal of Adolescent Health*, **67** (5), 730, https://doi.org/10.1016/j.jadohealth.2020.07.039.

Pacheco, J., Kuhn, I. and Grant, V. (2010) Librarians' Use of Web 2.0 in UK Medical Schools: Outcomes of A National Survey, *New Review of Academic Librarianship*, **16** (1), 75–86, https://doi.org/10.1080/13614531003597874.

Pangborn, S. M., Boatwright, B. C., Miller, C. L. and Velting, M. N. (2021 'I Don't Feel Like a Hero': Frontline Healthcare Providers' Social Media Storytelling during COVID-19, *Health Communication*, **38** (8),1508–18, https://doi.org/10.1080/10410236.2021.2017108.

Parvin, S. (2018) Propagating Your Story with Pinterest: Possibilities for Academic Libraries, *International Information and Library Review*, **50** (4), 328–35, https://doi.org/10.1080/10572317.2018.1526854.

Pastorino, R., De Vito, C., Migliara, G., Glocker, K., Binenbaum, I., Ricciardi, W. and Boccia, S. (2019) Benefits and Challenges of Big Data in Healthcare: An Overview of the European Initiatives, *European Journal of Public Health,* **29** (Supplement 3), 23–7, https://doi.org/10.1093/eurpub/ckz168.

Peach, B. C., Sole, M. L., Diaz, S. and Nunez, M. (2023) Screening Out False Participants in Research Recruitment from Social Media Groups, *American Journal of Nursing,* **123** (8), 52–5, https://doi.org/10.1097/01.NAJ.0000947476.62816.13.

Petrosyan, A. (2024) UK Daily Time Spent on Mobile 2021, *Statista,* www.statista.com/statistics/1285042/uk-daily-time-spent-mobile-usage.

Pinho-Costa, L., Yakubu, K., Hoedebecke, K., Laranjo, L., Reichel, C. P., Colon-Gonzalez, M. D., Neves, A. L. and Errami, H. (2016) Healthcare Hashtag Index Development: Identifying Global Impact in Social Media, *Journal of Biomedical Informatics,* **63**, 390–9, https://doi.org/10.1016/j.jbi.2016.09.010.

Piqueras-Sola, B., Cortés-Martín, J., Rodríguez-Blanque, R., Menor-Rodríguez, M. J., Mellado-García, E., Merino Lobato, C. and Sánchez-García, J. C. (2024) Systematic Review on the Impact of Mobile Applications with Augmented Reality to Improve Health, *Bioengineering (Basel),* **11** (6), 622, https://doi.org/10.3390/bioengineering11060622.

Potter, N. (2023) Where Should Libraries Go Now Twitter *HAS* Become a Wasteland?, www.ned-potter.com/blog/nomadic-social-media-part-2-libraries-in-the-post-twitter-age.

Prensky, M. (2001) Digital Natives, Digital Immigrants, *On the Horizon,* **9** (5), www.marcprensky.com/writing/Prensky%20-%20Digital%20Natives,%20Digital%20Immigrants%20-%20Part1.pdf.

Price, A.M., Devis, K., LeMoine, G., Crouch, S., South, N. and Hossain, R. (2018) First Year Nursing Students Use of Social Media Within Education: Results of a Survey, *Nurse Education Today,* **61**, 70–6, https://doi.org/10.1016/j.nedt.2017.10.013.

Priem, J., Groth, P. and Taraborelli, D. (2012) The Altmetrics Collection, *PLoS One,* **7** (11), https://doi.org/10.1371/journal.pone.0048753.

Priestman, W., Anstis, T., Sebire, I. G., Sridharan, S. and Sebire, N. J. (2019) Phishing in Healthcare Organisations: Threats, Mitigation and Approaches, *BMJ Health Care Informatics,* **26** (1), https://doi.org/10.1136/bmjhci-2019-100031.

Prince, N. J., Cass, H. D. and Klaber, R. E. (2010) Accessing E-Learning and E-Resources, *Medical Education,* **44** (5), 436–7, https://doi.org/10.1111/j.1365-2923.2009.03614.x.

Przybylski, A. K. and Weinstein, N. (2017) A Large-Scale Test of the Goldilocks Hypothesis: Quantifying the Relations Between Digital-Screen Use and the Mental Well-Being of Adolescents, *Psychological Science,* **28** (2), 204–15, https://doi.org/10.1177/0956797616678438.

Psychiatrist.com (2023) Viral TikTok 'Benadryl Challenge' Claims Life of 13-Year-Old Boy, www.psychiatrist.com/news/viral-tiktok-benadryl-challenge-claims-life-of-13-year-old-boy.

Pulido, C. M., Redondo-Sama, G., Sordé-Martí, T. and Flecha, R. (2018) Social Impact in Social Media: A New Method to Evaluate the Social Impact of Research, *PLoS One,* **13** (8), https://doi.org/10.1371/journal.pone.0203117.

Radcliffe Department of Medicine (2024) New Study Finds Semaglutide (or 'Ozempic/Wegovy') Safe for Brain Health with Possible Benefits for Cognition and Nicotine Dependence, www.rdm.ox.ac.uk/news/new-study-finds-semaglutide-or-2018ozempic-wegovy2019-safe-for-brain-health-with-possible-benefits-for-cognition-and-nicotine-dependence.

Ramasubramanian, S., Aujla, S., Raj, A., Pendyala, K. S. and Shivani, R. (2023) Trending Facts or Misinformation: A Study Determining Accuracy of Instagram Posts in the Context of Stroke Prevention and Management, *International Journal of Medical Science and Current Research,* **6**, 167–73, www.researchgate.net/publication/372588517_.

Ranemo, C. (2022) *Bibliotek 2022. Offentligt finansierade bibliotek,* Kungliga biblioteket, https://urn.kb.se/resolve?urn=urn:nbn:se:kb:publ-707.

Ranganathan, S. R. (1931) *The Five Laws of Library Science*, Madras Library Association and Edward Goldston, Ltd.

Ray, K. (2024) The History of Google Search – 1998 to 2023+, *Sitecentre®,* www.sitecentre.com.au/blog/history-of-google-search.

Regalado, A. (2011) Who Coined 'Cloud Computing'? *MIT Technology Review,* www.technologyreview.com/2011/10/31/257406/who-coined-cloud-computing.

Richard, L., Chiocchio, F., Essiembre, H., Tremblay, M. C., Lamy, G., Champagne, F. and Beaudet, N. (2014) Communities of Practice as a Professional and Organizational Development Strategy in Local Public Health Organizations in Quebec, Canada: An Evaluation Model, *Healthcare Policy,* **9** (3), 26–39, www.ncbi.nlm.nih.gov/pmc/articles/PMC3999567.

Rose, C. (2018) The Complete History of Search Engines, *SEO Mechanic,* www.seomechanic.com/complete-history-search-engines.

Rutter, J. (2020) Nudge Unit, *Institute for Government,* www.instituteforgovernment.org.uk/article/explainer/nudge-unit.

Saenger, A. K., Berkwits, M., Carley, S., Haymond, S., Ennis-O'Connor, M., Sherbino, J. and Smith, S. W. (2018) The Power of Social Media in Medicine and Medical Education: Opportunities, Risks, and Rewards, *Clinical Chemistry,* **64**, 1284–90, https://doi.org/10.1373/clinchem.2018.288225.

Salehan, M. and Negahban, A. (2013) Social Networking on Smartphones: When Mobile Phones Become Addictive, *Computers in Human Behavior,* **29** (6), https://doi.org/10.1016/j.chb.2013.07.003.

Samur, A. and Christison, C. (2018) The History of Social Media: 29+ Key Moments, *Hootsuite Social Media Management*, https://blog.hootsuite.com/history-social-media.

Sapp, L. and Cogdill, K. (2010) Blogging in Support of Health Information Outreach, *Medical Reference Services Quarterly*, **29** (3) 240–8, https://doi.org/10.1080/02763869.2010.494488.

Sarker, A., O'Connor, K., Ginn, R., Scotch, M., Smith, K., Malone, D. and Gonzalez, G. (2016) Social Media Mining for Toxicovigilance: Automatic Monitoring of Prescription Medication Abuse from Twitter, *Drug Safety*, **39** (3), 231–40, https://doi.org/10.1007/s40264-015-0379-4.

Schlegel, E. and Primacio, J. (2021) Blogging for the Continuum of Medical Education: Engaging Diverse Communities of Learners, *MedEdPublish*, **10**, 136, https://doi.org/10.15694/mep.2021.000136.1.

Schleicher, D., Jarvers, I., Kocur, M., Kandsperger, S., Brunner, R. and Ecker, A. (2024) Does it Need an App? – Differences Between App-Guided Breathing and Natural Relaxation in Adolescents after Acute Stress, *Psychoneuroendocrinology*, **69**, https://doi.org/10.1016/j.psyneuen.2024.107148.

Schwaab, J., Kman, N., Nagel, R., Bahner, D., Martin, D. R., Khandelwal, S., Vozenilek, J., Danforth, D. R. and Nelson, R. (2011) Using Second Life Virtual Simulation Environment for Mock Oral Emergency Medicine Examination, *Academic Emergency Medicine*, **18** (5), 559–62, https://doi.org/10.1111/j.1553-2712.2011.01064.x.

Scott, N. and Goode, D. (2020) The Use of Social Media (SoMe) as a Learning Tool in Healthcare Education: An Integrative Review of the Literature, *Nurse Education Today*, **87**, https://doi.org/10.1016/j.nedt.2020.104357.

Scullard, P., Peacock, C. and Davies, P. (2010) Googling Children's Health: Reliability of Medical Advice on the Internet, *Archives of Disease in Childhood*, **95** (8), 580–2, https://doi.org/10.1136/adc.2009.168856.

Seddon, S. (2023) Covid Inquiry: Read the Private WhatsApp Messages from inside Downing Street, *BBC News*, www.bbc.co.uk/news/uk-67275967.

Seh, A. H., Zarour, M., Alenezi, M., Sarkar, A. K., Agrawal, A., Kumar, R. and Khan, R. A. (2020) Healthcare Data Breaches: Insights and Implications, *Healthcare (Basel)*, **8** (2), https://doi.org/10.3390/healthcare8020133.

Servick, K. and Enserink, M. (2020) A Mysterious Company's Coronavirus Papers in Top Medical Journals May Be Unraveling, *Science*, www.science.org/content/article/mysterious-company-s-coronavirus-papers-top-medical-journals-may-be-unraveling.

Shajari, S., Kuruvinashetti, K., Komeili, A. and Sundararaj, U. (2023) The Emergence of AI-Based Wearable Sensors for Digital Health Technology: A Review, *Sensors (Basel)*, **23** (23), https://doi.org/10.3390/s23239498.

Sheerer, N. (2024) Engineering the Wireless Hospital: RF Issues, *Wi-Fi.org*, www.wi-fi.org/beacon/natalie-sheerer/engineering-the-wireless-hospital-rf-issues.

Shelley, M. W. (1818) *Frankenstein; or, The Modern Prometheus*, Lackington, Hughes, Harding, Mavor & Jones.

Sheridan, S. (2022) What Is Topic Modeling? A Beginner's Guide, *Levity*, https://levity.ai/blog/what-is-topic-modeling.

Shrestha, P., Sathanur, A., Maharjan, S., Saldanha, E., Arendt, D. and Volkova, S. (2020) Multiple Social Platforms Reveal Actionable Signals for Software Vulnerability Awareness: A Study of GitHub, Twitter and Reddit, *PLoS One*, **15** (3), https://doi.org/10.1371/journal.pone.0230250.

Sigerson, L. and Cheng, C. (2018) Scales for Measuring User Engagement with Social Network Sites: A Systematic Review of Psychometric Properties, *Computers in Human Behavior*, **83**, 87–105, https://doi.org/10.1016/j.chb.2018.01.023.

Sohn, M., Jeong, S. J., Kim, J. and Lee, H. J. (2017) Crowdsourced Healthcare Knowledge Creation Using Patients' Health Experience-Ontologies, *Soft Computing*, **21** (2), https://doi.org/10.1007/s00500-017-2529-3.

Solli, K. and Ødemark, I. L. (2019) Multilingual Research Writing Beyond English: The Case of Norwegian Academic Discourse in an Era of Multilingual Publication Practices, *Publications*, **7** (2), 25.

Soni, J. (2020) *NHS Bans Staff from Using Zoom over Privacy Concerns. TechRadar*, www.techradar.com/news/nhs-bans-staff-from-using-zoom-over-privacy-concerns.

Springer, S., Zieger, M. and Strzelecki, A. (2021) The Rise of Infodemiology and Infoveillance during COVID-19 Crisis, *One Health*, 100288, https://doi.org/10.1016/j.onehlt.2021.100288.

Sprout Social (2020) *Social Media Demographics to Inform your Brand's Strategy in 2020*, https://sproutsocial.com/insights/new-social-media-demographics.

Starr, S. (2011) The Librarian in the Cloud: or Beware of Unintended Consequences, *Journal of the Medical Library Association*, **99** (4), 267–9, https://doi.org/10.3163/1536-5050.99.4.001.

Stephens, T. M. and Gunther, M. E. (2016) Twitter, Millennials, and Nursing Education Research, *Nursing Education Perspectives*, **37** (1), 23–7.

Stringhini, G., Wang, G., Egele, M., Kruegel, C., Vigna, G., Zheng, H. and Zhao, B. Y. (2013) Follow the Green, *Proceedings of the 2013 Conference on Internet Measurement Conference*, https://doi.org/10.1145/2504730.2504731.

Suarez-Lledo, V. and Alvarez-Galvez, J. (2021) Prevalence of Health Misinformation on Social Media: Systematic Review, *Journal of Medical Internet Research*, **23**, https://doi.org/10.2196/17187.

Subramaniam, M., Koh, Y. S., Sambasivam, R., Samari, E., Abdin, E., Jeyagurunathan, A., Tan, B. C. W., Zhang, Y., Ma, S., Chow, W. L. and

Chong, S. A. (2024) Problematic Smartphone Use and Mental Health Outcomes Among Singapore Residents: the Health and Lifestyle Survey, *Asian Journal of Psychiatry*, **98**, https://doi.org/10.1016/j.ajp.2024.104124.

Suen, K., Zhang, R. and Kutaiba, N. (2024) Accuracy of Wrist Fracture Detection on Radiographs by Artificial Intelligence Compared to Human Clinicians: A Systematic Review and Meta-Analysis, *European Journal of Radiology*, **178**, https://doi.org/10.1016/j.ejrad.2024.111593.

Suomi, R., Mäntymäki, M. and Söderlund, S. (2014) Promoting Health in Virtual Worlds: Lessons from Second Life, *Journal of Medical Internet Research*, **16** (10), e229, https://doi.org/10.2196/jmir.3177.

Sutherland, S. and Jalali, A. (2017) Social Media as an Open-Learning Resource in Medical Education: Current Perspectives, *Advances in Medical Education and Practice*, **8**, 369–75, https://doi.org/10.2147/AMEP.S112594.

Syn, S. Y. (2023) Gaze Movement Analysis Examined How People View and Interact with Health Information on Facebook Pages, *Health Information and Libraries Journal*, 1–15, https://doi.org/10.1111/hir.12497.

Tagliabue, F., Galassi, L. and Mariani, P. (2020) The 'Pandemic' of Disinformation in COVID-19, *SN Comprehensive Clinical Medicine*, **2**, 1287–9, https://doi.org/10.1007/s42399-020-00439-1.

Tattersall, A. (2011) How the Web was Won . . . By Some, *Health Information and Libraries Journal*, **28** (3), 226–9, https://doi.org.1111/j.1471-1842.2011.00945.x.

Tattersall, A., Beecroft, C. and Cantrell, A. (2011) Using Web 2.0 Tools to Create Customized Research Portals, *Journal of Electronic Resources in Medical Libraries*, **8** (4), 367–81, https://doi.org/10.1080/15424065.2011.626346.

Taylor, K. A. and Humphrey, W. F. Jr. (2021) Impact of Medical Blog Reading and Information Presentation on Readers' Preventative Health Intentions: Mixed Methods, Multistudy Investigation, *Journal of Medical Internet Research*, **23** (12), https://doi.org/10.2196/23210.

Taylor & Francis Librarian Resources (2014) *Use of Social Media by the Library*, https://librarianresources.taylorandfrancis.com/insights/library-advocacy/use-social-media-by-the-library.

Thaung, C. (2018) Blogging for Medical Education – a Personal View, *Journal of the Royal College of Physicians of Edinburgh*, **48** (1), 48–9, https://doi.org/10.4997/JRCPE.2018.112.

Thelwall, M. and Thelwall, S. (2020) A Thematic Analysis of Highly Retweeted Early COVID-19 Tweets: Consensus, Information, Dissent and Lockdown Life, *Journal of Information Management*, **72** (6), 945–62, https://doi.org/10.1108/AJIM-05-2020-0134.

Thielst, C. B. (2010) *Social Media in Healthcare: Connect, Communicate, Collaborate*, Health Administration Press.

Topolovec-Vranic, J. and Natarajan, K. (2016) The Use of Social Media in Recruitment for Medical Research Studies: A Scoping Review, *Journal of Medical Internet Research*, **18** (11), e286, https://doi.org/10.2196/jmir.5698.

Topping, A. (2009) 'Web 2.0' Declared Millionth Word in English Language, *The Guardian*, www.theguardian.com/books/2009/jun/10/english-million-word-milestone.

Tsapatsoulis, N. and Djouvas, C. (2019) Opinion Mining From Social Media Short Texts: Does Collective Intelligence Beat Deep Learning? *Front Robot AI*, **5**, 138, https://doi.org/10.3389/frobt.2018.00138.

Twitter (2020) About Twitter, https://about.twitter.com

University System of Georgia (n.d.) A Brief History of the Internet, www.usg.edu/galileo/skills/unit07/internet07_02.phtml.

van der Boon, R. M. A., Camm, A. J., Aguiar, C., Biasin, E., Breithardt, G., Bueno, H., Drossart, I., Hoppe, N., Kamenjasevic, E., Ladeiras-Lopes, R., McGreavy, P., Lanzer, P., Vidal-Perez, R. and Bruining, N. (2024) Risks and Benefits of Sharing Patient Information on Social Media: A Digital Dilemma, *European Heart Journal of Digital Health*, **5** (3), 199–207, https://doi.org/10.1093/ehjdh/ztae009.

van Doren, T. P. (2021) The 1918 Influenza Pandemic Has Lessons for COVID-19: An Anthropology Student Perspective, *American Journal of Public Health*, **111** (1), 79–80, https://doi.org/10.2105%2FAJPH.2020.306021.

van Kampen, K., Laski, J., Herman, G. and Chan, T. M. (2022) Investigating COVID-19 Vaccine Communication and Misinformation on TikTok: Cross-Sectional Study, *JMIR Infodemiology*, **2** (2), https://doi.org/10.2196/38316.

Van Noorden, R. (2023) More than 10,000 Research Papers were Retracted in 2023 – a New Record, *Nature*, **624** (7992), 479–81, https://doi.org/10.1038/d41586-023-03974-8.

Vanzetta, M., Dal Molin, A., Vellone, E., Alvaro, R., Arrigoni, C. (2016) Social Media and Nurse Education: An Integrative Review of the Literature, *Annali di Igiene: Medicina Preventiva e di Comunita*, **28** (3), 187–201, https://doi.org/10.7416/ai.2016.2097.

Vassilakaki, E. and Garoufallou, E. (2015) The Impact of Twitter on Libraries: A Critical Review of the Literature, *Electronic Library*, **33** (4), 795–809, https://doi.org/10.1108/EL-03-2014-0051.

Ventola, C. L. (2014a) Social Media and Health Care Professionals: Benefits, Risks, and Best Practices, *Pharmacy & Therapeutics*, **39**, 491–520, www.ncbi.nlm.nih.gov/pmc/articles/PMC4103576/pdf/ptj3907491.pdf.

Ventola, C. L. (2014b) Mobile Devices and Apps for Health Care Professionals: Uses and Benefits, *Pharmacy & Therapeutics*, **39** (5), 356–64, www.ncbi.nlm.nih.gov/pmc/articles/pmid/24883008.

Viewsourcecode (2025) RedHanded: Sneaking Ruby Through the System: Stop, for Blogging's Sake,

https://viewsourcecode.org/why/redhanded/inspect/tumbleloggingAssortedLarvae.html.

von Muhlen, M. and Ohno-Machado, L. (2012) Reviewing Social Media Use By Clinicians, *Journal of the American Medical Informatics Association,* **19** (5), 777–81, https://doi.org/10.1136/amiajnl-2012-000990.

Vosoughi, S., Roy, D. and Aral, S. (2018) The Spread of True and False News Online, *Science,* **359**, 1146–51, https://doi.org/10.1126/science.aap9559.

Vukušić Rukavina, T., Viskić, J., Machala Poplašen, L., Relić, D., Marelić, M., Jokic, D. and Sedak, K. (2021) Dangers and Benefits of Social Media on E-Professionalism of Health Care Professionals: Scoping Review, *Journal of Medical Internet Research,* **23**, https://doi.org/10.2196/25770.

Waddell, D. C., Barnes, M. and Khan-Kernahan, S. (2012) Tapping into the Power of Twitter: A Look at Its Potential in Canadian Health Libraries, *Partnership: The Canadian Journal of Library and Information Practice and Research,* **7** (2), https://journal.lib.uoguelph.ca/index.php/perj/article/view/1999/2624.

Walsh, L. E. and Carter-Bawa, L. (2023) Using Social Media to Recruit Individuals for Health-Related Research: Feasibility and Lessons Learned, *Journal of Health Psychology,* **28** (7), 599–606, https://doi.org/10.1177/13591053221136928.

Wan, S. H. (2017) The Pokémon Go Effect to Motivate Healthy Behavior Changes, Take Some Cues from Pikachu and Co, *Minnesota Medicine,* **100** (2), 28–30.

Ware, S. A., Howe, P. S. and Scalese, R. G. (2000) Interactive Reference at a Distance: A Corporate Model for Academic Libraries, *Reference Librarian,* **69/70**, 171–9, www.ariadne.ac.uk/issue/77/prince-jacon-igwe.

Wellman, M. L., Stoldt, R., Tully, M. and Ekdale, B. (2020) Ethics of Authenticity: Social Media Influencers and the Production of Sponsored Content, *Journal of Media Ethics,* **35** (2), 68–82, https://doi.org/10.1080/23736992.2020.1736078.

Wenger, E. (1998) *Communities of Practice: Learning, Meaning, and Identity,* Cambridge University Press.

Whitney, W., Keselman, A. and Humphreys, B. (2017) Libraries and Librarians: Key Partners for Progress in Health Literacy Research and Practice, *Studies in Health Technology and Informatics,* **240**, 415–32, www.ncbi.nlm.nih.gov/pmc/articles/PMC5724359.

WHO (World Health Organization) (n.d.) WHO Campaigns, www.who.int/campaigns.

Wicks, P., Massagli, M., Frost, J., Brownstein, C., Okun, S., Vaughan, T., Bradley, R. and Heywood, J. (2010) Sharing Health Data for Better Outcomes on PatientsLikeMe, *Journal of Media Internet Research,* **12** (2), e19, https://doi.org/10.2196/jmir.1549.

Wiggins III, R. H. (2004) Personal Digital Assistants, *Journal of Digital Imaging,* **17**, 5–17, https://doi.org/10.1007/s10278-003-1665-8.

Wikipedia (2025) Truth Social, https://en.wikipedia.org/wiki/Truth_Social.

Williams, N. A. (2022) Personal Librarian Programs in Medical and Academic Health Sciences Libraries: A Preliminary Study, *Journal of the Medical Library Association,* **110** (1), 87–96, https://doi.org/10.5195/jmla.2022.1290.

Williams, T. A. and Duell, M. (2020) NHS Staff Criticised for Dancing, *Mail Online,* www.dailymail.co.uk/news/article-8245313/Fury-endless-showreel-NHS-staff-dancing-fooling-coronavirus-crisis.html.

Willis, E., Friedel, K., Heisten, M., Pickett, M. and Bhowmick, A. (2023) Communicating Health Literacy on Prescription Medications on Social Media: In-depth Interviews With 'Patient Influencers', *Journal of Medical Internet Research,* **25**, e41867, https://doi.org/10.2196/41867.

Winder, D. (2007) Back to Basics: Social Networking, *Information World Review,* **23** (28).

Wojtara, M. S. (2023) Use of Social Media for Patient Education in Dermatology: Narrative Review, *JMIR Dermatology*, 6, e42609, https://doi.org/10.2196/42609.

Wolfe, S., Hu, S., Rundle, C. W., Weintraub, G. and Dellavalle, R. P. (2021) Healthcare Ethics and Professionalism in Social Media. In Bercovitch, L., Perlis, C. S., Stoff, B. K. and Grant-Kels, J. M. (eds) *Dermatoethics*, 185–97, Springer, https://doi.org/10.1007/978-3-030-56861-0_20.

Wood, H. (2017) T&F Buys Reference-Management Tool Colwiz, *The Bookseller,* www.thebookseller.com/news/tf-buys-reference-management-tool-colwiz-560936.

Wood, M. S. (1991) Public Service Ethics in Health Sciences Libraries, *Library Trends,* **40** (2), 244–57, https://core.ac.uk/download/pdf/4817109.pdf.

Woodward, M. (2024) Twitter User Statistics 2024: What Happened after 'X' Rebranding?, *Search Logistics,* www.searchlogistics.com/learn/statistics/twitter-user-statistics.

World Bank (2011) World Development Indicators – Google Public Data Explorer, www.google.com/publicdata/explore?ds=wb-wdi&met=it_net_user&idim=country%3ACHN&dl=en&hl=en&ref=troyhunt.com#.

Worldometer (2025) *World Population by Year – Worldometers,* www.worldometers.info/world-population/world-population-by-year.

Xavier, D., Miyawaki, I., Campello Jorge, C. A., Freitas Silva, G. B., Lloyd, M., Moraes, F., Patel, B. and Batalini, F. (2024) Artificial Intelligence for Triaging of Breast Cancer Screening Mammograms and Workload Reduction: A Meta-Analysis of a Deep Learning Software, *Journal of Medical Screening,* **31** (3), 157–65, https://doi.org/10.1177/09691413231219952.

Yalamanchili, B., Donelle, L., Jurado, L. F., Fera, J. and Basch, C. H. (2022) Investigating #covidnurse Messages on TikTok: Descriptive Study, *Journal of Medical Internet Research Nursing,* **5** (1), https://doi.org/10.2196/35274.

Yeung, A., Ng, E. and Abi-Jaoude, E. (2022) TikTok and Attention-Deficit/Hyperactivity Disorder: A Cross-Sectional Study of Social Media

Content Quality, *Canadian Journal of Psychiatry*, **67** (12), 899–906, https://doi.org/10.1177/07067437221082854.

Young, S. N. (2008) The Neurobiology of Human Social Behaviour: An Important but Neglected Topic, *Journal of Psychiatry and Neuroscience*, **33** (5), 391–2,

Young, J. C., Boyd, B., Yefimova, K., Wedlake, S., Coward, C. and Hapel, R. (2020) The Role of Libraries in Misinformation Programming: A Research Agenda, *Journal of Librarianship and Information Science*, **53** (4), 539–50, https://doi.org/10.1177/0961000620966650.

Younger, P. and Morgan, P. (2011) *Using Web 2.0 for Health Information*, Facet Publishing.

Zenone, M., Ow, N. and Barbic, S. (2021) TikTok and Public Health: A Proposed Research Agenda, *BMJ Global Health*, **6** (11), https://doi.org/10.1136/bmjgh-2021-007648.

Zhang, B. (2023) Prompt Engineers or Librarians? An Exploration, *Medical Reference Services Quarterly*, **42** (4), 381–6, https://doi.org/10.1080/02763869.2023.2250680.

Zhou, L., Zhang, D., Yang, C. and Wang, Y. (2018) Harnessing Social Media for Health Information Management, *Electronic Commerce Research and Applications*, **27**, 139–51, https://doi.org/10.1016/j.elerap.2017.12.003.

Zohoorian-Fooladi, N. and Abrizah, A. (2013) Academic Librarians and Their Social Media Presence, *Information Development*, **30** (2), 159–71, https://doi.org/10.1177/0266666913481689.

Zotti, F., Zotti, R., Albanese, M., Nocini, P. F. and Paganelli, C. (2019) Implementing Post-Orthodontic Compliance Among Adolescents Wearing Removable Retainers through Whatsapp: A Pilot Study, *Patient Preference and Adherence*, **13,** 609–15, https://doi.org/10.2147/PPA.S200822.

Index